I0130056

Fiscal Policy within the IS-LM Framework

Fiscal Policy within the IS-LM Framework

Shahdad Naghshpour

business**expert**
Press

Fiscal Policy within the IS-LM Framework
Copyright © Business Expert Press, LLC, 2014.

All rights reserved. No part of this publication may be reproduced, stored in a retrieval system, or transmitted in any form or by any means—electronic, mechanical, photocopy, recording, or any other except for brief quotations, not to exceed 400 words, without the prior permission of the publisher.

First published in 2014 by
Business Expert Press, LLC
222 East 46th Street, New York, NY 10017
www.businessexpertpress.com

ISBN-13: 978-1-60649-722-7 (paperback)
ISBN-13: 978-1-60649-723-4 (e-book)

Business Expert Press Economics Collection

Collection ISSN: 2163-761X (print)
Collection ISSN: 2163-7628 (electronic)

Cover and interior design by Exeter Premedia Services Private Ltd., Chennai, India

First edition: 2014

10 9 8 7 6 5 4 3 2 1

Printed in the United States of America.

To Emily

SN

Abstract

Governments have become an integral part of economics in modern societies. The extent of government involvement is not limited to legislation, foreign policy, or law and order. Governments intervene in economic affairs by collecting taxes and spending what they collect. The amount of taxes and who pays them, as well as the amount of government expenditures and who receives them, has a significant impact on income distribution. However, the main focus of the study of fiscal policy is on the overall economic impact of government involvement in the economy, instead of its distributional effects. While we know that when a person is taxed his or her utility is reduced, and when someone receives a payment, either because of selling something to the government or in the form of transfer payment, that person's utility increases. However, economic theory is not able to determine what happens to social utility when one person is taxed and another person receives the government payment. By not addressing the utility effect of government intervention in the economy the need for finding an answer to what happens to collective utility vanishes and allows us to focus on what happens to aggregate economic measures when the government intervenes in economic activities.

In a democratically elected government the purpose of fiscal policy is to accommodate the will of the people. Big governments are the people's response to powerful multinational companies, many of which have more revenue than most governments. Another role of government is to reduce social injustice by establishing a safety net for the less fortunate. Transfer payments and social safety nets have been developed for two completely different reasons. One reason has been the yearning for social justice and compassion for fellow human beings. An equally important reason has been to reduce inequality in order to avoid social unrest in protest to unpleasant living conditions.

The subject of this book is about how government intervention affects economic aggregates, such as unemployment, economic growth, and inflation. The effort has been to provide a discussion in the tradition of positive economics and to avoid normative arguments. The question here is not whether government should intervene in the economy, whom should be taxed, or which sector of the economy should be assisted.

Instead, the focus is on how government involvement in the economy affects its course and the consequences of such interventions. The collective response of economic agents to economic and noneconomic factors is the expected outcome of the economy, which is formulated as economic theory. Economic theory is not wishful thinking of economists or a purposeful design of a person or a group to create a desired product as in many areas. For example, computers are designed and created to accomplish a set of desired outcomes. Economics, on the other hand, is understanding how economic agents react to factors that affect the economy. Economic theories reflect how the economy functions and what causes changes. Therefore, they are explaining the reality, which is the result of the interaction of people in response to changes in economic and social factors. It is not necessary for an economic agent to know economics in order to comply with economic theory any more than it is necessary for a planet to know the laws of physics to "choose" an appropriate orbit and speed for its position among other planets, with respect to its star. In this context the source of changes in economy is irrelevant; it can be endogenous, or exogenous. Whether government intervention is endogenous or exogenous is a totally different argument.

Keywords

fiscal policy, interest rate, IS schedule, LM schedule, monetary policy, liquidity

Contents

List of Figures

Acknowledgments

I am indebted to my family for the time I took away from them. I would like to thank Candace Bright, Brian Carriere, Charles Tibedo, and Michael Webb, all doctoral students in the International Development and International Affairs Program at the University of Southern Mississippi. The following people have graciously provided helpful comments, corrections, and proof-reading parts of the text: Richard T. Baker, III, CPA Business Division Chair, Copiah-Lincoln Community College; Edward R. Bee of Taimerica Management Company; Gregory A. Bonadies, Principal Resurrect, LLC; Shawn Low; Pat R. O'Brien, Donald G. Soderquist College of Business John Brown University. Without their assistance, I would not have been able to finish this book. Their contributions have been essential, and without their tireless efforts I would not have been able to finish this work. Any remaining shortcomings rest solely on my shoulders.

SECTION I

Background and Fundamental Theories

CHAPTER 1

A Brief History of Fiscal Theory

It is seldom possible to pinpoint the birth of an idiom, or know exactly when a term was coined. However, in the case of macroeconomics we are able to do that. The term "macroeconomics" was coined by Klein in 1946, in an article titled "Macroeconomics and the Theory of Rational Behavior."

Definition

Macroeconomics is the study of aggregated indicators, such as gross domestic product (GDP).

Definition

GDP is the value of final goods and services produced in a country in one year.

The conduct of governments in modern economies affects aggregate economic indicators. The influence of government on the economy is often deliberate, for example, when taxes are increased to reduce budget deficits. Sometimes the purpose of government action is not to influence the economy but rather for other causes, such as improving the welfare of orphans or supporting single mothers through social security payments. Regardless of the purpose of government action, GDP is still affected. Government intervention in the economy for the purpose of changing aggregate indicators falls into two distinct forms: fiscal policy and monetary policy.

Definition

Fiscal Policy refers to government intervention in the economy through manipulation of government revenues and disbursements, for the purpose of influencing the course of the economy.

Definition

Monetary Policy refers to government intervention in the economy through manipulation of supply of money, for the purpose of influencing the course of the economy.

Whether the government should intervene in the economy is a normative question. This book does not address the wisdom of government intervention in the economy; instead, it focuses on the effects of government interventions on the economy. More specifically, it focuses on the impact of taxes and expenditures on macroeconomic indicators.

The branch of economics that covers these subjects is called macroeconomics. The fact that the term was not devised until 1946 does not mean that the concept was not in use before this time. Macroeconomics is a formal way of addressing economic aggregates such as the price level, unemployment rate, national product, and the like. The coverage of macroeconomic topics for the first two centuries of modern economics was sparse, and it was usually based on microeconomic perspectives. In fact, addressing larger scale issues, such as inflation, full employment, aggregate output, and a possible role for government to use fiscal and monetary tools to influence them, did not exist until 1936, when John Maynard Keynes published *The General Theory of Employment, Interest, and Money*. Keynes's work was timely because of the Great Depression of 1929. During the Great Depression the free market system was not able to correct itself and cause a return to the full employment.

Definition

An economic **recession** refers to an overall decline in an economy. In the United States a recession is declared when GDP declines for two consecutive quarters.

Definition

An economic **depression** is a severe case of a recession.

Most but not necessarily all economic activities decline during a recession. A prolonged decline in the economy is necessary to conclude that a recession exists, since short-term fluctuations in the economy are common.

The Great Depression was the most severe depression of the modern era. By most accounts, the Great Depression began in late summer of 1929 and became acute in October 1929, when the stock market in the United States crashed. The Depression spread to most industrialized countries, and its effects were still present as late as 1939. During the Great Depression, reductions in production, prices, and trade were substantial. Unemployment was high and widespread in industrialized countries. The economic decline during the Great Depression surpassed all recessions in the recorded history of the last several centuries.

What Is Fiscal Theory?

It seems logical to refer to the theories that provide economic justifications for fiscal policy as fiscal theory. However, the term is not commonly used. The concept of fiscal policy is closely related to the notion of aggregate product and income. The theories that are applicable to fiscal policy are covered in the domain of macroeconomics. The theoretical foundation of fiscal theory is covered under the subject of income determination. In its simplest form the theory is based on the fact that national income consists of the aggregate income of each sector of the economy. Similar entities are grouped together. Consumer expenditures are grouped together and represent **consumption** (C). The other groups represent **investment** (I), **government expenditures** (G), and **foreign trade**. Foreign trade consists of two components; **imports** (M) and **exports** (X). Customarily, **net trade** is utilized (X – M). The sum of consumption, investment, government expenditures, and net trade constitutes aggregate expenditure. Since expenditure by one person is income for another person, aggregate expenditure is identical to aggregate income.

There is a subtle difference between GDP and gross national product (GNP). The former consists of all goods and services produced in a country, regardless of the nationality of the producer. The latter is the value of all goods and services produced by the citizens of a country, regardless of their location of residency. Until 1991, GNP was the primary measure of aggregate productivity in the United States. Using GDP instead of GNP accomplished two things. First, it provided a better measure of the productivity of the nation since it is based on the use of resources in the country. Second, it allowed a more accurate comparison of productivity of the United States with other countries, since GDP is more commonly used.

Early Fiscal Theories

By most accounts, Keynes originated the theory of income determination. There is little doubt that the inability to avoid the Great Depression, or at least slow it down, was essential in prompting economists to realize that a solution based on something other than monetary theory is necessary to soften the troughs and peaks of business cycles. Business cycles existed before that time period and were studied by Sismondi as early as 1819. However, Frisch often receives credit for starting macroeconomics, since he used the term "macrodynamic" in his study of economic cycles.[1]

The existence of business cycles was problematic for classical economists. According to Adam Smith, the invisible hand allocates resources to products that are demanded and away from products that are not. Under classical economics, disequilibrium is a temporary situation, during which the invisible hand is busy reallocating resources to their best use, in order to maximize the utilities of consumers and the profits of producers. An important point to remember is that the foundation of classical economics originated in microeconomics, since macroeconomics was not formally established for another 200 years. Under classical economics, disequilibrium is a temporary condition, and the likelihood that all economic sectors are out-of-equilibrium is low. Business cycles contradict these beliefs. Studies of business cycles first emerged in the 18th century (Hume)[2] and 19th century (Fisher and Wicksell).[3-5]

Classical economists used to blame business cycles on exogenous factors, such as wars or natural disasters. An alternative was to focus on the long run, thus eliminating the issue of disequilibrium, which they did extensively. Owen and Sismondi attributed business cycles to overproduction and under-consumption, which were brought about by wealth inequality.[6] Sismondi might have been the first economist to advocate governmental intervention under a capitalistic system to end business cycles, which became known as fiscal policy in the 20th century, while Owen advocated socialism instead. Neither idea gained much support among the classical economists, although a stronger case for socialism was made by Marx, in *Das Kapital*.[7] Sometimes the advocates of fiscal policy are called socialists in the United States. However, there is a major difference between Marx and Keynes. The former is suggesting a revolution to end capitalism, while the latter is proposing an evolution to make the capitalist system work when the invisible hand fails.

Neoclassical Macroeconomics

While classical economists advanced the economic frontier more than all their predecessors, they failed to explain some basic issues. Notable among them and pertinent to the discussion on hand is the existence of business cycles, which, according to Marx, provide proof of the fallacy of Say's Law of the Market.[8]

Definition

Say's Law of the Market states that production creates its demand.

In other words, production generates sufficient income to create enough demand for all goods and services produced in an economy. According to Say, "products are paid for by products." This statement is in essence a macroeconomic statement. Say's Law links production in one industry to demand generated by income created by other industries. While it is possible to produce too little or too much in one industry or sector, it is not possible to do so at the level of national economy. Aggregate demand and aggregate supply are not independent from each other; they are determined endogenously. In microeconomics the determinants of demand are different than the determinants of supply, which makes them independent of each other. Therefore, what is true at the microeconomic level need not be necessarily true, and often is not, at macroeconomic level. In a barter economy, supply and demand are related, even at microeconomic level.

Definition

Barter is the exchange of one good for another when neither good is "money."

The critical missing element in a barter economy is the money. Lack of money forces demand to be equal to supply at both the macroeconomic and microeconomic levels. For more detail about money and barter economies, the reader is referred to Naghshpour.[9] Overproduction and underproduction require a point of reference for comparison, a role served by money, which does not exist in a barter economy. Hence, in barter economies, aggregate production must equal aggregate demand, but this is not necessarily so in an economy that functions via money. In order to have an excess supply of something there must be an excess demand for something else. However, in a barter economy it is impossible to have an excess supply over demand for all goods. A general oversupply of commodities in a monetary economy implies there is an excess demand for money. This situation indicates disequilibrium, which cannot be a permanent condition.

One implication of Say's Law is that the money market is always in equilibrium because money is only used for exchange; goods are supplied to demand other goods. Patinkin refers to this relationship as the "dichotomized pricing process," whereby classical and neoclassical economists use relative prices in the commodity market (homogeneity postulate) and absolute prices (i.e., nominal) in the money market.[10] These aggregate analyses became the foundations of macroeconomics and the center point of the IS-LM analysis, which is covered in Chapter 3. Say's Law is in fact a valid comparative static case. However, this is exactly the main point of Keynes's opposition to Say's Law, since full equilibrium is a dynamic process. Full equilibrium is pursued constantly; however, it is never achieved. The process of pursing equilibrium may in fact displace the equilibrium point.

Why *Laissez Faire* Is Abandoned?

Adam Smith uses the self-interest motive to demonstrate that the removal of trade restrictions would be advantageous.[11] The interest of a society is believed to be the sum of the interests of its individuals. When a person maximizes his utility, the utility of the entire society is maximized, as if an invisible hand orchestrates the necessary processes. To maximize social wealth, individuals should be allowed to seek their fortunes the way they see fit. When individuals pursue their self-interest, whether they are persons or firms, they compete with each other. Therefore, uninhibited competition is the same as the invisible hand. Perfect competition ensures the efficient allocation of resources in their best use that maximizes each individual's welfare, and thus, that of the society as a whole. Smith subscribes to the "spontaneous harmony of interests" doctrine, which claims that a "spontaneous order" results from individuals' pursuit of their self-interest; an unintended social consequence is maximization of the social welfare. Competition equalizes the rates of return for labor and capital among firms, as well as industries, and eliminates excess gains. Thus, it causes efficient allocation of resources. However, in the same chapter, Smith defends the existence of the Navigation Laws, and supports protectionism in the case of infant industries or as a retaliatory measure. The 18th century was the era of *laissez faire*, but not because of Smith's influence on policymakers. The doctrines that advocated government intervention had already faded by the time the *Wealth of Nations* was written.

Definition

Laissez faire et laissez passer is a doctrine that opposes government intervention in economic affairs, except for the maintenance of property rights.

Le Gendre, a French businessman, is credited for uttering the first part of the phrase, in response to the question of how the French government could help commerce. Le Gendre's statement is a reflection of the overall atmosphere in Europe toward government's role in the economy in the late 17th century, even in France where mercantilism ruled. The second part of the phrase was added by Gournay in mid-eighteenth century, to promote free trade. Smith referred to the doctrine of a "balance of trade," which prevailed between the end of the 16th century and the middle of the 18th century. The groups that are representatives of mercantilism are known as Physiocrats, although they referred to themselves as *les economists*.

In modern times, and in light of the fact that most governments in the 21st century account for a large portion of their national GDP, which in the case of the United States has been as high as 37% GDP (e.g., in 2009), the issue has become a matter of the extent of government involvement rather than the concept itself. Sometimes the degree of allegiance to the concept is influenced by the self-interest of the proponents. For example, many of the governments from developed countries that advocate free trade in the 21st century supported trade barriers and government involvement in the economy at earlier stages of their economic development. Similar contradictory stances can be cited from private organizations. For example, the *Economist*, an ardent advocate of free trade and *laissez faire*, supported the Corn Laws that imposed tariffs on cereals, in spite of an ongoing famine in Ireland in 1845.

Fisher points out that the extreme *laissez faire* doctrine held by classical economists had been replaced by the doctrine of governmental regulation and social control.[12] He acknowledges that the change to the latter had been gradual, and that it was not due to the emergence of a rival doctrine, but rather because of practical limitations of the doctrine of *laissez faire*. Fisher was familiar with Marx's *Das Kapital*; however, Marxism was not practiced in any country in 1907.[13] Nevertheless, Fisher points out that "[S]ocialism cannot be put in practice without opposition, and to maintain itself socialism must hold the opposing class in subjection."

According to Fisher, one reason for the popularity of *laissez faire* from the 16th to 18th century was the weakness of governments. With the emergence of stronger governments there was less support for the doctrine. Another cited reason was that industries, especially the railroads, had become very powerful, and governments had to react to survive and to protect the public's interests and rights. The inability of governments to deal with powerful and wealthy corporations proved disastrous in Latin America and underdeveloped countries in other regions as late as the third quarter of the 20th century. These and similar issues are political in nature, and Fisher states that he would rather focus on economic reasons for the shift. However, his discussion concentrates mostly on either the common sense of avoiding poor practices, such as indiscriminate spitting, or on issues relating to social welfare, such as the virtue of humanitarian societies, like the American Institute of Social Service. Fisher attributes the failure of *laissez faire* to people's lack of ability to know what constitutes their best interest, but he admits that sumptuary laws are ill-advised.

From an economic perspective the demise of *laissez faire* lay in its inability to explain business cycles, especially its recession component.

The invisible hand is supposed to allocate resources to assure their most efficient use and to maintain equilibrium, except in brief transitory periods, which occur after external shocks and before the economy reaches a new equilibrium. By definition, *laissez faire* cannot allocate resources efficiently when there are externalities.

Definition

Externalities are consequences, both positive and negative, that were not brought about by one's own choice and action.

At the level of individuals, one might receive a positive externality from a neighbor's flower bed; a utility gain at zero cost. One might receive a negative externality from a neighbor's noisy party, or construction. At the firm level, externalities are present in similar fashions. A classic example, dating to the early days of the Industrial Revolution, is demonstrated by the smoke of a factory falling on the laundry service of a neighboring firm. Since the polluting factory does not have to pay for the cost of cleaning, it will overproduce its product due to the negative externality. On the other hand, goods with positive externalities, such as education, are underproduced in a competitive market. In the presence of externalities, the invisible hand is incapable of moving resources from one industry to another to maximize social welfare.

Laissez faire will also fail when there are economies of scale. The economy of scale exists when the unit cost of production decreases with increases in production. It can be shown that the short run average cost curve falls with an increase in production, reaches a minimum, and then increases afterward. It can also be shown using microeconomic production theory that firms do not operate in the declining segment of their short-run average cost curves. When a particular level of output is feasible on the declining segment of the curve, the next unit of output must also be feasible, because it costs less. However, the concept of economy of scale is based on the long-run average cost curve. When the long-run average cost of an industry is declining, a firm can eliminate its competitors by choosing to expand its production; consequently, one firm can produce sufficient amounts for the entire market, hence creating a monopoly.

Definition

Economy of scale exists when the long run average cost is declining, that is, per unit cost declines as output increases.

Definition

Monopoly is a market structure in which a single producer provides the good or service. For instance, a single bank in a small town is a monopoly.

In such cases the *laissez faire* approach fails and history has shown that people tend to look to the government to intervene.

CHAPTER 2

Politics and Fiscal Policy

Keynes is the founder of the notion of fiscal policy; his work in the wake of the Great Depression established fiscal policy as a viable tool for macroeconomic policy.[1] Previously, the only way the government deliberately influenced the economy was through monetary policy. Government involvement in money affairs began the first time a government minted a coin. However, government involvement in the economy at the time of the Great Depression was limited to coinage on the monetary front and collection of taxes to pay for government expenditures; an act that is part of fiscal policy in modern economics. However, these actions were not used as policy instruments. Additionally, the modern notion of monetary policy started, or at least became official, with the establishment of the first central bank in Sweden. There, in 1668, the Riksbank was established to lend money to the government, although the concept of monetary policy was firmly in place by the time the Bank of England was created in 1694, established as a joint stock company in order to buy government debt. In 1913, the United States established its central bank, the Federal Reserve Bank (Fed), to end its financial calamities.[2] By the time of the Great Depression (1929–1939), monetary policy for the purpose of affecting the course of the economy was well established in industrial countries. However, before delving into the politics of fiscal policy it is necessary to introduce some monetary terminologies.

Definition

Easy money refers to abundance of money and credit at low interest rates.

Definition

Tight money refers to shortage of money and credit and the presence of high interest rates.

Shortcomings of Monetary Policy

In the aftermath of the stock market crash in October 1929, and the onset of the Great Depression, the economies of the industrialized countries experienced low interest rates. According to monetary theory and historical evidence, low interest rates are a consequence of an abundance of money, which makes it cheap. The central banks of many countries, most notably the Federal Reserve Bank of the United States, interpreted this as the need to tighten the money supply. Tight money is contractionary because it raises interest rates and reduces investment. While this prescription is suitable for inflationary periods, it is not helpful during recessions, let alone for the greatest of all recessions in history.

The interest rate is only one economic factor that explains economic conditions. A low interest rate, other things being equal, signals an easy money environment. However, other things were not equal during the Great Depression. There was ample and clear evidence that output had fallen, and that prices were lower than before. These indicators signify a tight money environment. The fact that the interest rate was low was the consequence of the easy monetary policy of the Fed during the 1920s. The focus on interest rates misled the Fed to adopt a contractionary monetary policy, hence worsening and prolonging the depression. Friedman and Schwartz acknowledge that the Fed's actions were not appropriate for the economic conditions of the Great Depression and attribute its conduct to the lack of a suitable replacement following the death of Benjamin Strong in 1928, who had been the Governor of the Federal Reserve and Chairman of the Open Market Investment Committee.[3] However, there are dissenting views. Wicker[4] rejects Friedman and Schwartz's conclusions, and Brunner and Meltzer point out that Strong did not have a countercyclical policy.[5] Alternatively, Epstein and Ferguson state there was no mistake, and claim the Fed's contractionary policy was deliberately aimed at achieving the market correction it deemed necessary and also to protect commercial banks, even at the expense of the national economy or welfare of the citizens.[6] Anderson, Shughart, and Tollison offer a more cynical view, claiming that the Fed seized the moment to bankrupt non-member banks.[7]

The reality of the existence of the Great Depression forced the Fed to adopt easy monetary policy in order to lower the interest rate, which was already low at the time. Hayek accused the Fed of prolonging the depression by this action.[8] This view is also shared by George Norris, Governor of the Federal Reserve Bank of Philadelphia, as noted in the minutes of the June 23, 1930, meeting of the Open Market Committee report. Keynes was not happy with this diagnosis and offered an alternative explanation for the presence of low interest rates and a completely new remedy to end recessions; namely fiscal policy.[9] Friedman and Schwartz, however, argues that the closures of banks reduced the supply of available money due to loss of deposits that could no longer be loaned.[10] Therefore, the Fed should have increased the supply of money instead of decreasing it, to compensate for the decline in available money. In other words, the Fed should have taken an expansionary monetary policy to offset the contractionary impact of the loss of money due to bank closures. According to Friedman, the easy money policy was the correct measure but its magnitude was not sufficient. This argument fails to explain the existence of low interest rates during this era.

A New Explanation

Keynes's analysis begins with the fundamental question of why money is demanded. The classical answer was that money is demanded to pay for transactions. Keynes calls this the transaction motive for demand for money. He introduces two other motives; the precautionary motive and speculative motive.[11] The speculative motive of the demand for money is important for the discussion on hand. In the absence of inflation, money does not lose its value; however, it does not earn any interest either. On the other hand, some assets, such as treasury bonds, earn interest, in addition to maintaining their value. The value of some assets, such as stocks, fluctuates over time. Yet other securities pay dividends and appreciate in value as well. The type, timing, and nature of payment, determines the specific name for the resulting revenue, such as interest, yield, or dividend.

The timing of transactions in interest bearing assets is important. In order to make profit from these financial instruments, one should buy when their prices are low and sell when their prices are high. Unfortunately, it is not possible for everyone to buy low and sell high. The expectation of what will happen to a specific stock in the future is not the same for all people. This difference stems from the fact that individuals possess varying levels of information, tolerances for taking risks, and the availability of other options, or the necessity to have cash. This is because expectations about the future, the availability of resources, and information about assets are different for buyers and sellers. The seller must expect the asset price to fall in the future, while the buyer must believe the opposite. Similarly, the seller might need cash, believe that another asset provides higher return, or need to change his portfolio mix, thus making it reasonable to sell his assets. The opposite must be true for the buyer. Therefore, the disparity of needs, expectations, opportunities, and information make it possible for people to buy and sell assets at a given price. The prices of traded assets fluctuate in response to the expectations and needs of buyers and sellers. When there are more buyers than sellers, prices increase, while the opposite is true when the number of sellers exceeds the number of buyers. Furthermore, the amount of cash available to different people varies over time. Younger people tend to be borrowers while older people tend to be lenders, other things being equal. When a transaction does take place, the exchange price must be the same for the buyer and the seller.

The expectation of what will happen in the future is an important factor in the decision to buy or sell assets. For example, an expectation of a price decline initiates the need to sell, even if the current price is below the price of the original purchase. In such cases, the asset holder is minimizing his loss. We deliberately avoid using the word "profit" as much as possible, because it has a different meaning in economics. As will be explained in Chapter 8, the correct term is "earning income from assets." An anticipation of a price increase would prompt a purchase, which requires having cash on hand to take advantage of the opportunity. There are two ways to have sufficient cash to make a transaction. First, one could hold extra cash balances over and beyond the amount necessary to meet one's transaction needs. Second, one could sell or liquidate other assets to obtain the necessary cash. Keynes termed this the **portfolio** or **speculative motive**.[12] According to this motive, changes in economic conditions and/or stock prices affect the amount of money people choose to hold. Changes in the amount of money people hold also changes velocity of money, and invalidates the constancy of velocity, a key assumption held by the advocates of the quantity theory. Furthermore, since converting assets to money in anticipation of possible bargains in the stock market is costly and time-consuming, the decision to change the amount of money held as cash must be made when possible and appropriate. To convert a low yield asset into a higher yield asset, one must first convert the existing asset into money, which is then exchanged for the new asset. Thus, decisions to increase the amount of cash on hand are not made at regular intervals, which imply a non-constant velocity of money.

Liquidity Trap

When interest rate is low, people expect it to rise in the future; therefore, the demand for money based on the speculative motive increases accordingly. At sufficiently low interest rate such as was witnessed during the Great Depression, the overall expectation is that interest rate will increase; thus, the demand for money increases without limit, or as economists prefer to say, the elasticity of demand with respect to the interest rate becomes infinite. Keynes named this perfectly elastic demand for money the **liquidity trap**. Under such circumstances, people would demand an insatiable amount of cash balances. In the presence of liquidity trap, monetary policy becomes completely ineffective because increases in supply of money cannot lower the interest rate any further, since it is practically zero. Further, it cannot increase investment because expectations are that stock prices will decline in response to the increase in interest rate. This argument provides a plausible explanation of the observed behavior of interest rates and economic conditions during depressions.

According to Keynes's analysis, during such periods people would not choose to hold any bonds. Alternatively, people would not hold any cash when their expectations are that interest rates will decrease. Empirical evidence does not support either extreme in these "all or nothing" scenarios.[13] Another problem with Keynes's explanation is that if interest rates stay low for a long time, peoples' expectations would change and the speculative demand for money would end.[14] Tobin overcomes the first problem by accounting for the possibility that people hold both money and bonds.[15] His model assumes the existence of the risk of capital gain or loss, due to uncertainty about future interest rates. The extent of holding bonds depends on an individual's desire to earn interest versus his ability to tolerate risk, as well as his expectations about future interest rates. This model is closer to reality, due to the possibility of portfolio diversity.

Fiscal Policy as an Alternative to Monetary Policy

After providing a plausible explanation for low interest rates during the Great Depression and the ineffectiveness of the monetary policy, Keynes proposed that the government should intervene and stimulate the economy.[16] The quickest and most potent way to end a recession is deficit financing. Deficit financing refers to the situation in which government spends more than it collects in taxes. When a government spends a dollar, someone's income increases by one dollar. According to Keynes, the individual will use part of that income for consumption, while saving the rest for other purposes, such as for speculation in the stock market. He refers to the former as marginal propensity to consume (MPC).

Definition

Marginal Propensity to Consume is the change in consumption due to a one unit change in income.

The MPC is assumed to be positive, indicating that at least part of a change in income is used for consumption, and less than one, which implies that consumption out of additional income does not exceed the extra income; it also implies that part of the additional income is saved. By assumption, saved income is invested. However, even at zero income, it is still necessary to consume some positive amount to survive, which is represented by C_0 in the consumption model. Although the MPC is customarily used in reference to consumers, one can think of the MPC for a government as well. It can be argued that when a government has a budget deficit, its MPC is greater than one.

Multiplier Effect

Keynes points out that MPC is affected by "a change in the wage-unit, a change in the difference between income and net income, a change in the rate of time-discounting, changes in fiscal policy, and changes in expectations of the relation between the present and the future level of income."[17] He also argues that part of annual investment replaces worn-out equipment, and hence does not increase the productive capacity of the economy. Failure to replace depreciated equipment reduces the production capacity and causes a decline in national wealth due to decline in gross domestic product (GDP). Originally, the concept of a multiplier was introduced through a change in investment because a change in production capacity is the only way to increase output, employment, and income. However, a change in any of the components of national income, namely C, I, G, and X-M, would have similar effect. Under a reasonable assumption of constancy of the MPC for the duration of the analysis the multiplier effect can be demonstrated in the following way.

An initial one dollar increase in investment generates $MPC new income in the second round. Of this new income MPC percent is spent and the rest is saved. Therefore, in the third round $MPC new income is generated the process continues indefinitely. As a numerical example assume that MPC = 0.9 and the initial increase in expenditure is $100. Incomes in successive rounds would be:

Round 1: 100,000,000
Round 2: 100,000,000 × 0.9 = 90,000,000
Round 3: 90,000,000 × 0.9 = 81,000,000
Round 4: 81,000,000 × 0.9 = 72,900,000
Round 5: 72,900,000 × 0.9 = 65,610,000

The sum of all money created by this process will be equal to

$$(1/(1 - 0.9)) \times 100{,}000{,}000 = \$1{,}000{,}000{,}000$$

Since MPC = 0.9, the multiplier effect is equal to 1/ (1 − 0.9) = 1/0.1 = 10.

A smaller MPC produces a smaller multiplier effect. When the MPC = 0.8, the new income generated in round five is $40,960,000 instead of $65,610,000 because the multiplier is five instead of ten: 1/(1 − 0.8) = 1/0.2 = 5. When investment does not increase as a result of recession, governments can stimulate the economy through deficit financing. Thus, Keynes demonstrates that in order to increase GDP by $1 billion, it is only necessary to spend $100 million in deficit financing, provided that the MPC is 0.9.

Economic Case Against Fiscal Policy

Until the 1930s, discretionary fiscal policy did not exist. Prior to the 1930s, fiscal policy referred to the regulations and theories for tax collection. The argument against government waste may in fact date to the dawn of civilization, as it seems careless spending of other people's money is a human trait, which is called moral hazard. However, the problem arises, in part, from the fact that the utility from consumption differs among people and the same product does not increase the utility of everyone by equal amount. Therefore, even when government expenditures are based on maximizing the utility of the majority of taxpayers the decisions will fail to maximize the utilities of the rest of taxpayers, and thus, a source of complaints about government wastefulness.

The *General Theory* created substantial research on the topic. Ironically, some of Keynesian economics' major proponents, such as Tobin, were also its major critics. One can argue that their critique was to improve the doctrine, as they did not oppose it. The main opposition came from Milton Friedman in many of his works. The criticism was not necessarily confined to fiscal policy since Friedman argues that the major problems with discretionary policy, fiscal or monetary, stem from the inability to detect the problem in time, prescribe the correct remedy, and then administer the correct dose.[18] These issues are augmented by problems of inside and outside lags.

Definition

An **inside lag** is the time between recognition of the need for a stimulus or restraint and the legislation of the appropriate regulations.

Definition

An **outside lag** is the time between a policy action and the appearance of its effects in the economy.

Political Case Against Fiscal Policy

The political case against fiscal policy is normative and based on the opponents' view that "small government" is better. The issue of government is also a recurring theme. Since the last quarter of the 20th century, due to a persistent budget deficit in the United States, the attitude of the general public is more negative toward government spending. In light of the fact that many of the opponents do not wish to cut certain expenditures, such as defense, Medicare, and at least parts of Social Security, it seems that the main target of their criticisms is the transfer payments and social programs. The United States has always been less inclined than European countries to support social programs such as extended unemployment benefits or higher education. It is easier for an economist to understand oppositions, such as to government expenditure, as long as it is possible to identify the economic reason. For example, the protest of people who are subject to the higher tax rates is based on loss of utility. However, when people with lower incomes oppose government expenditures, the view is primarily normative and based on philosophical opinions.

CHAPTER 3

Two Blades Are Better Than One: The Role of IS-LM

IS-LM analysis is an important tool that acknowledges the need for equilibrium in the goods and the money markets simultaneously in order for equilibrium to prevail in an economy. To avoid undue complexity, equilibrium in each market is presented separately and then combined for the final analysis. Both markets rely on the interest rate to provide necessary signals for investment and lending decisions.

Definition

The **IS schedule** is the loci of interest rate output sets for which the goods market is in equilibrium.

Definition

The **LM schedule** is the loci of combinations of interest rates and incomes that result in equilibrium in the money market.

Aggregate Demand

The goods market represents total production, which is used to satisfy demand from different sectors. Aggregate demand arises from the sum of individual **consumption** (C), **investment** (I) by firms, **government expenditures** (G), and **foreign trade**. Foreign trade consists of two components, **imports** (M) and **exports** (X). Customarily **net trade** is utilized $(X - M)$ and is represented by NX below. Therefore, aggregate demand (Y) is the sum of all demands by all sectors:

$$Y = C + I + G + \text{NX} \qquad (3.1)$$

Inclusion of government expenditures is misleading because it does not indicate how the government obtains the funds it spends. Assume government generates funds though taxation only. Taxes reduce consumption and should be included in the consumption function, which will be incorporated below.

Equations such as 3.1 do not provide any information about the nature of each variable and how they are determined. It is possible to assume that all the components of the right-hand side are determined without regard to economic conditions; in other words, they are exogenous variables. This is a common practice in elementary economics. The right-hand side variables in equation 3.1 are exogenous since they are not specified in terms of internal forces of the economy. More realistically, each variable can be expressed in terms of the factors that influence it. For example, it is reasonable to express consumption as a function of income, a fact that is implied by the marginal propensity to consume (MPC). In the presence of taxes and **transfer payments** (TP), consumption is a function of disposable income, instead of income.

Definition

Disposable income is gross income minus taxes plus TP.

Recall that "aggregate income," by definition, is equal to "aggregate output." For the sake of brevity the word "aggregate" is omitted when there is no ambiguity. For a more realistic model the source of government revenue, that is taxes, must be incorporated. Taxes reduce disposable income while TP increase it. Let the tax rate (t) be constant and assume TP are exogenous, shown by (TP_0). In a progressive tax system, multiple tax rates exist and the rates increase with income. Progressive taxes complicate computations without adding anything to the analysis, therefore, for the sake of clarity only the constant rate is presented in equation 3.3. Furthermore, assuming a constant component for tax (T_0) that is independent of income would make it easier to discuss the effect of balanced budget multipliers later.

$$Y_d = Y - T + \text{TP}_0 \tag{3.2}$$

$$T = T_0 + tY \qquad 0 < t < 1 \qquad\qquad (3.3)$$

In order to survive, a subsistence level of consumption is necessary (C_0). However, as disposable income increases consumption is expected to increase proportionately, according to the magnitude of the MPC. Therefore, consumption can be expressed as:

$$C = C_0 + cY_d \qquad 0 < c < 1 \qquad\qquad (3.4)$$

where c is the MPC. Substitute for Y_d from equation 3.2 in equation 3.4 to obtain the results

$$C = C_0 - c\,T_0 + c\,\mathrm{TP}_0 + c\,(1 - t)\,Y \qquad 0 < c, t < 1 \qquad\qquad (3.5)$$

Similarly, investment can be expressed in terms of an autonomous component and the interest rate. It is customary to assume a portion of investment is independent from the interest rate as well as income (I_0). Higher interest rates mean greater costs for a given amount of investment. Therefore, there is an inverse relationship between interest rates and investment. The relationship between the autonomous investment and interest rate is presented in the following equation:

$$I = I_0 - bi \qquad b > 0 \qquad\qquad (3.6)$$

where b is responsiveness of investment to interest rate. Substituting the relationships expressed in equations 3.5 and 3.6 into equation 3.1 results in the following:

$$Y = C_0 - cT_0 + c\mathrm{TP}_0 + c(1 - t)\,Y + I_0 - bi + G_0 + \mathrm{NX} \qquad (3.7)$$

For simplicity, government expenditure is assumed to be exogenous, which is represented by G_0. Endogenous government expenditure would make the analysis slightly more complex but provides no additional explanatory power to the model. Foreign trade is excluded for ease of computation. This exclusion implies a balanced trade where imports equal exports. Rearrange known and unknown variables to obtain:

$$Y[1 - c(1 - t)] = C_0 - cT_0 + cTP_0 + I_0 + G_0 - bi \qquad (3.8)$$

Let $A = C_0 + cTP_0 + I_0 + G_0$ represent all the constants. Move all the unknowns to the left side of the equation and factor them out.

$$[1 - c(1 - t)]\, Y = A - bi \qquad (3.9)$$

$$Y = \frac{A}{1 - c(1 - t)} - \frac{b}{1 - c(1 - t)} i \qquad (3.10)$$

Equation 3.10 is useful in explaining the IS schedule as well as the multiplier effect. Equation 3.10 presents the multiplier effect of a change in interest rates on income, assuming everything else remains the same.

Multiplier Effect

Let one of the factors that are constant to change from state zero to state one. Factors that affect the constants are exogenous, that is, they are not influenced by economic forces. Instead, they change due to noneconomic causes such as changes in taste. For example, suppose government expenditures changes from G_0 to G_1. Replace A with its components to be able to trace the changes in government expenditures. In state zero, output is Y_0, shown in equation 3.11, and in state one it is Y_1, shown in equation 3.12.

$$Y_0 = \frac{C_0 - cT_0 + cTP_0 + I_0 + G_0}{1 - c(1 - t)} - \frac{b}{1 - c(1 - t)} i \qquad (3.11)$$

$$Y_1 = \frac{C_0 - cT_0 + cTP_0 + I_0 + G_1}{1 - c(1 - t)} - \frac{b}{1 - c(1 - t)} i \qquad (3.12)$$

The difference in the two states is the change in output in response to changes in the government expenditures.

$$Y_1 - Y_0 = \frac{1}{1 - c(1 - t)}(G_1 - G_0) \tag{3.13}$$

The magnitude $k = \dfrac{1}{1 - c(1 - t)}$ is the multiplier effect. Since both c and t are between zero and one the magnitude of k is greater than one.

The multiplier in the case of endogenous consumption, investment, and taxes is equal to k. Let MPC = 0.9 and the tax rate = 0.2; a $1,000,000,000 increase in government expenditures will increase the output/income by

$$
\begin{aligned}
Y_1 - Y_0 &= [1/(1 - 0.9(1 - 0.2))] \times 1,000,000,000 \\
&= [1/(1 - 0.72)] \times 1,000,000,000 \\
&= [1/0.28] \times 1,000,000,000 \\
&= 3.571428571 \times 1,000,000,000 \\
&= \$3,571,428,571
\end{aligned}
$$

Balanced Budget Multiplier

In the above example the government expenditures increase as if by magic. In real life the increase must be funded in some way. One possibility is to fund government expenditures through deficit financing. An alternative way is to increase taxes to equal the increase in expenditures. The multiplier in the case of deficit financing is the same as described above. When taxes are increased to pay for the additional government expenditures the government is using balanced budget on new expenditures, therefore both G and T must change by equal amounts. Assuming that the government increases the exogenous portion of the taxes without increasing the tax rate equation 3.13 becomes

$$Y_1 - Y_0 = \frac{1}{1 - c(1 - t)}(G_1 - G_0) - \frac{c}{1 - c(1 - t)}(T_1 - T_0) \tag{3.14}$$

Since the increase in expenditures is equal to the increase in taxes $(G_1 - G_0) = (T_1 - T_0)$ the multiplier is:

$$k = \frac{1 - c}{1 - c(1 - b)} = \frac{1 - 0.9}{1 - 0.9(1 - 0.2)} = \frac{0.1}{1 - 0.72} = \frac{0.1}{0.28} = 0.357142857$$

Therefore, the same $1billion increase in government expenditures offset by the same amount of taxes will increase output/income by $357,143,857. Although the magnitude of the multiplier k decreases substantially in balanced budget expenditure, the income increases as a result of a new stimulus. The multiplier effect of the balanced budget is 10 times smaller than that of deficit financing in this example.

Figure 3.1 provides a visual presentation of the change in income as a result of a change in government expenditure. A change in government expenditures by the magnitude of $(G_1 - G_0)$ shifts aggregate expenditure up from $C + I + G_0$ to $C + I + G_1$. As a result, income increases from Y_0 to Y_1.

As a result of a change in G the economy is jolted out of its initial equilibrium point of E_0 towards point A. Since, at point A, the economy is not at equilibrium there is excess demand pressuring output to increase towards point B. The mechanism by which this occurs is through price changes. As a result of the increase in output income increases proportionately to the MPC, causing the economy to move in the direction of point C. The cycle repeats and the economy moves toward point D, until the economy reaches the new equilibrium point E_1. Note that at each successive round the increase in income and the pursuing consumption becomes smaller.

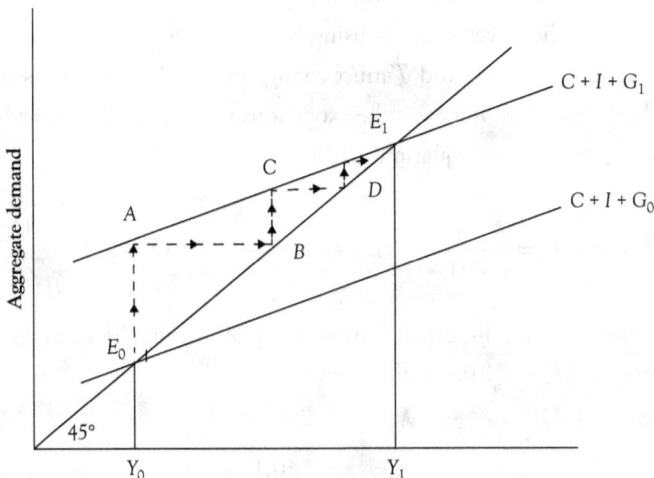

Figure 3.1. Changes in output as a result of a shift in government expenditures.

IS Schedule

The starting point for deriving the IS schedule is the endogenous investment function of equation 3.6, which relates investment to the interest rate. The relationship between investment and interest rates is believed to be inverse, which is represented by a negative sign in front of coefficient b; the responsiveness of investment to the interest rate. Figure 3.2 depicts the investment function. Technically, the equation represents the planned investment. However, at equilibrium, planned, and actual investments are equal. The values of income and aggregate demand are equal along the forty-five degree line.

As is evident in panel A of Figure 3.2, a decrease in the interest rate from i_0 to i_1 will cause an increase in investment from I_0 to I_1. However, an increase in investment will shift aggregate demand upward from $C + I_0 + G$ to $C + I_1 + G$, which results in an increase in income/output from Y_0 to Y_1, as shown in panel B of Figure 3.2.

The change in the interest rate also affects savings. Since whatever is not consumed is saved, equation 3.4 implies:

$$S = - C_0 + (1 - \text{MPC}) \ Y \qquad (3.15)$$

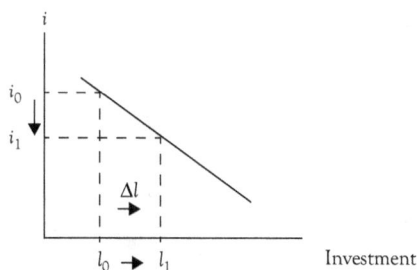

Panel A

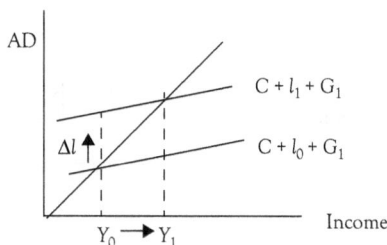

Panel B

Figure 3.2. Investment function.

Since savings must be equal to investment at equilibrium, the change in investment due to a change in the interest rate can be transferred to the savings function. Figure 3.3 depicts the top part of Figure 3.2 in panel A. Panel B of the graph simply transfers the changes in investment to their equivalent changes in savings in panel C. This takes places via the equilibrium condition of $I = S$ in panel B, which is simply the 45° line that transfers movements along the investment line to that of the savings line. Panel C provides the link between saving and income. From panel A any change in the interest rate changes the investment that can be tracked to panel D to find changes in income. Assuming all other factors remain constant in the goods market, the change in investment is the only factor that affects output. Transferring the two interest rates i_0 and i_1 from panel A to panel D provides the necessary information about the interest rate needed to determine the change in income. Transmitting the two incomes from panel C to panel D provides information about income. The intersection of these two sets of information provides two points in the interest-income plane in panel D. The resulting IS schedule is the loci of equilibrium points in the goods market for different levels of interest rates.

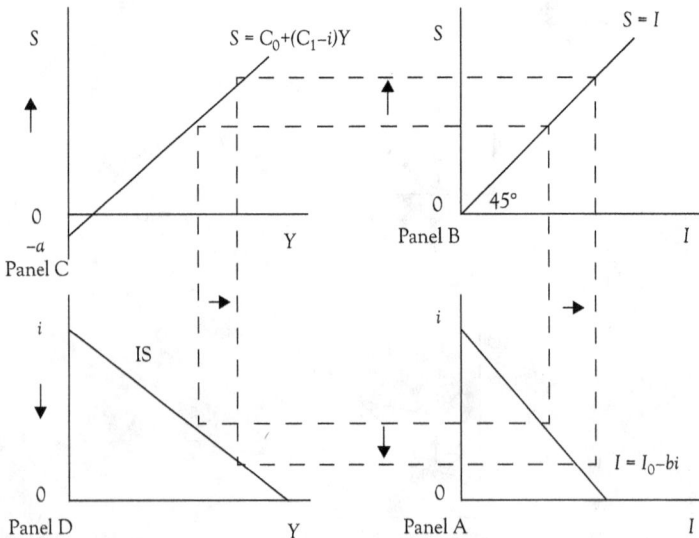

Figure 3.3. Derivation of the IS schedule.

The magnitude of the change in income in panel D of Figure 3.3 is the same as the shift in panel B of Figure 3.2.

LM Schedule

The demand for money is a function of two variables: the interest rate and income. For derivation of the LM schedule refer to Naghshpour.[1] The LM schedule depicts the relationship between income and the interest rate. Changes in demand for money cause disequilibrium in the money market, which causes changes in the interest rate. Changes in the interest rate change investment and balance the money market. The effect of changes in the money market is related to income via the LM schedule.

Equilibrium in the Goods and Money Market

The IS schedule depicts the points along which pairs of interest rates and income levels result in equilibrium in the goods market. The LM schedule depicts the points at which pairs of the interest rate and income are at equilibrium in the money market. Combining these, as in Figure 3.4, provides the unique pair of income and corresponding interest rate, where both the goods and money markets are at equilibrium. This corresponds to the intersection of the two curves, similar to the intersection of supply and demand in a single market case.

In order to determine the derivations of the IS and LM schedules, we made the simplifying assumption of constant prices and the ability of producers to increase their output without the need for a price increase. These assumptions are usually the characteristics of an underemployed

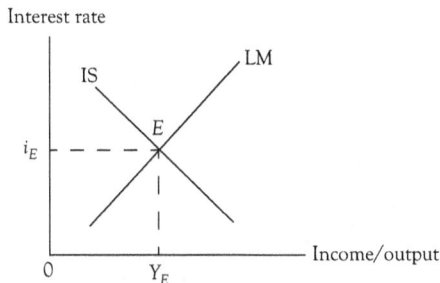

Figure 3.4. IS-LM schedule and market equilibrium.

and underutilized economy, which prevails during a recessionary period. Technically, except for when the economy is at full employment, there is always excess capacity. There is excess capacity when an economy slows down, when it is in recession, and during recovery. The constancy of price in this analysis is not the same as the perfectly elastic demand curve faced by a firm operating in a perfectly competitive market. The latter pertains to a single firm and is a microeconomics issue, while the constancy of price due to the existence of unemployment in the economy is a macro-economic problem.

The slopes of the IS and LM curves determine the extent of the responsiveness of the goods and money markets to changes in the interest rate. Many, if not all, contentions regarding the effectiveness of fiscal and monetary policies can be expressed in terms of the slopes of the IS and LM curves.

Effectiveness of Fiscal and Monetary Policies

The effectiveness of fiscal and monetary policies depends on the slopes of the IS and LM curves. The IS schedule is downward sloping, indicating that a decrease in the interest rate will increase investment, and hence, output through:

$$Y = C + I + G + (X - M)$$

Since the interest rate is not represented on either axis of the aggregate demand–aggregate supply diagram, the result of a change in the interest rate appears as an upward shift in the aggregate demand. At the new equilibrium, output will be higher to match the increased demand. Derivation of the IS schedule in this chapter is graphical. An algebraic derivation of the schedule based on equation 3.10 can also be utilized. Equation 3.6 indicates that a change in the interest rate changes investment, while equation 3.7 relates this change in investment to changes in output. This causes a movement along the IS curve. The magnitude of the move is a function of multiplier effect, which depends on the MPC and the tax rate. Recall that higher tax rates reduce the multiplier effect while increases in MPC increase it. Output can also change due to change in the magnitude of any of the constant factors grouped together in the first part of the equation. A change in these variables would cause a shift in the IS schedule.

Changes in subsistence levels or the autonomous part of investment would also shift the IS curve. However, these changes are of little interest to economists because they are affected by institutional factors and change gradually, if at all. More importantly, however, is the fact that they cannot be changed by policymakers; therefore, they are not policy instruments. The main fiscal policy tools are taxes and government expenditures, either for purchases or in the form of TP. Reductions in taxes increase consumers' disposable income, while tax increases have the opposite effect. Increases in government expenditures or TP increase aggregate expenditures; increasing gross domestic product (GDP) as a result.

When a change in taxes is matched by an equal change in government expenditures, the net result is a change in output in the same direction as, and equal to, the balanced budget multiplier. To achieve a greater impact on GDP, or due to political reasons, a government might decide to change its expenditures without changing taxes. The multiplier effect of deficit financing is much greater than the balanced-budget multiplier. In the example provided earlier the magnitude was 10 times greater for deficit financing multiplier than that of the balanced budget. Note that changes in the tax rate have a different impact than changes in the exogenous taxes that are not determined by income, such as excise taxes. A change in the former will cause a shift in the IS schedule as well as aggregate demand. A change in the latter will change the multiplier, thus changing the magnitude of the impact of multiplier.

An Increase in Government Expenditures

An increase in government expenditures shifts the IS curve to the right, by the same magnitude. The equilibrium point of E_0 in Figure 3.5 is no longer sustainable. The increase in expenditure increases income by the multiplier effect, thus income increases by $Y_1 - Y_0 = k(G_1 - G_0)$ where subscripts zero and one refer to the initial and final positions, respectively. The increase in income increases aggregate demand and income from the initial equilibrium point of E_0 to E'_0. The new, higher income level and aggregate demand increase the demand for money, which itself results in a switch from storing money in an interest-earning portfolio to holding money as cash. Changing from a portfolio to cash reduces the price of interest-earning assets and increases the interest rate. This increase in the interest rate reduces consumption and investment and causes a movement along the new IS_1 line from E'_0 to E_1, which reestablishes equilibrium at higher level of income. This analysis is solely based on the changes in the goods market, keeping the money market constant. However, the Fed can intervene in the market and change the interest rate. The discussion of the effects of changes in money market is the subject of monetary policy.[2]

Part of the crowding out effect occurs as a result of an increase in investment in response to an increased demand for goods, which results from an increase in government expenditures. An increase in demand for investment causes the interest rate to increase. A prerequisite for crowding out is that the economy must be at full employment. When idle capacity exists in the economy the increase in aggregate demand can be met without the need to increase investment. The interest rate can still increase as a result of an increase in demand for liquidity.

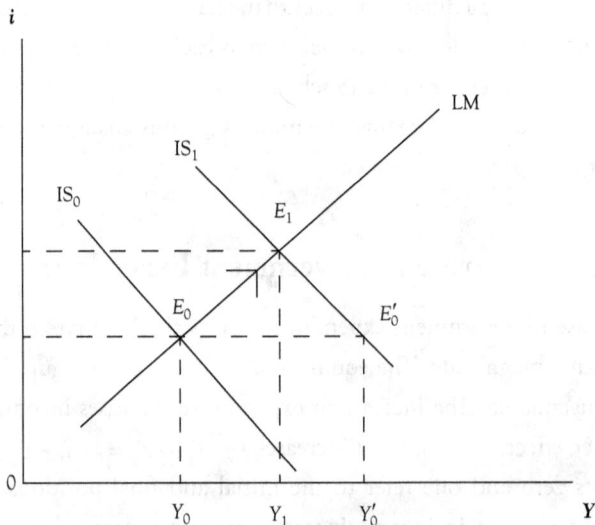

Figure 3.5. Effect of an increase in government expenditure.

Definition

Crowding out refers to an increase in interest rate as a result of expansionary fiscal policy.

The extent of the increase in output and aggregate demand depends on the slope of the IS schedule. A vertical IS will not have any decline after the initial increase, although the interest rate will still increase. The extent of the crowding out is a function of the LM schedule. When LM is flat the interest rate will not increase as a result of expansionary fiscal policy regardless of the slope of the IS schedule. A flat LM combined with a vertical IS represents the maximum effectiveness of fiscal policy.

Classical Economics and Crowding Out

Classical economists argue that the demand for money is determined by the value of transactions (QP) and is not affected by the interest rate. Consequently, the demand for money is interest inelastic and the LM schedule is vertical. An increase in government expenditures increases the interest rate, which causes enough reduction in investment to offset the expansionary effect of government expenditures, without any increase in output or income, as depicted in Figure 3.6. The case of a vertical LM

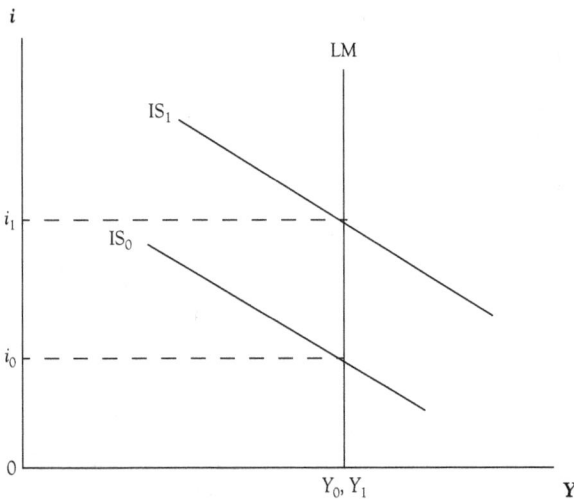

Figure 3.6. Vertical LM and ineffectiveness of fiscal policy (crowding out).

makes fiscal policy ineffective because an expansionary fiscal policy will cause the interest rates to increase without any increase in output. Fiscal policy is the least effective when a flat IS schedule is combined with a vertical LM schedule.

Liquidity Trap and Fiscal Policy

Liquidity trap was defined in Chapter 2 as the case where a decrease in the interest rate fails to increase investment. Consequently, the economy cannot return to full-employment equilibrium. In the presence of a liquidity trap the demand for money is perfectly elastic, which translates into a horizontal LM curve. When interest rates are low enough to create a liquidity trap, an expansion in government expenditures does not cause an increase in the interest rate. Therefore crowding out does not occur and fiscal policy is more effective. The fiscal policy would be at its maximum potential if the IS schedule is also vertical. The policy implication is that stimuli are more effective when there is a liquidity trap and the interest rate is very low, such as during a recession. The presence of liquidity trap makes the impact of fiscal policy stronger, regardless of whether government expenditures are increased or decreased. Therefore, expenditure

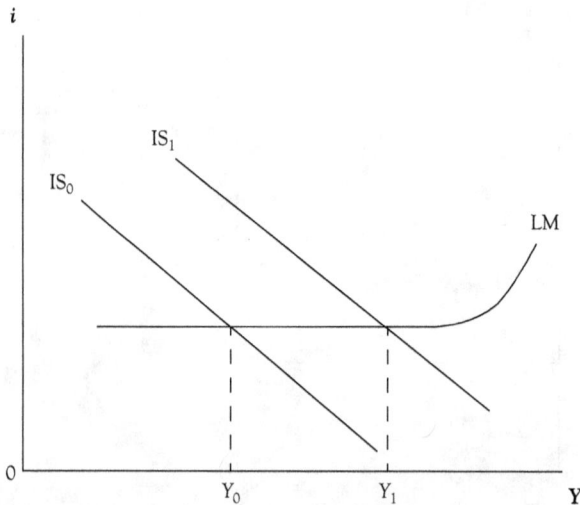

Figure 3.7. Horizontal LM and maximum effectiveness of fiscal policy (liquidity trap).

cuts during a recession would be detrimental to the economy. Figure 3.7 depicts the effect of an increase in government expenditures in the presence of liquidity trap.

The existence of liquidity trap must be accompanied by two other conditions for the above argument to be valid. First, investment must have a low interest elasticity. Therefore, lower interest rates will hardly result in an increase in investment. Second, labor should prefer to be unemployed than accept lower wages. Resistance to a decline in wages is sometimes called sticky wages.

Horizontal IS

For any given LM schedule a horizontal IS schedule would make fiscal policy more effective. Figure 3.8 presents the case. When the IS curve is horizontal the MPC is large and the multiplier effect is even stronger. A large MPC makes the slope of the aggregate demand steeper, which in turn result in a flatter IS schedule. The largest value for the MPC is one, under which consumers do not save any of their income. Lack of savings also implies a lack of investment, which could be possible in the short run because depreciated machinery must be replaced in the long run.

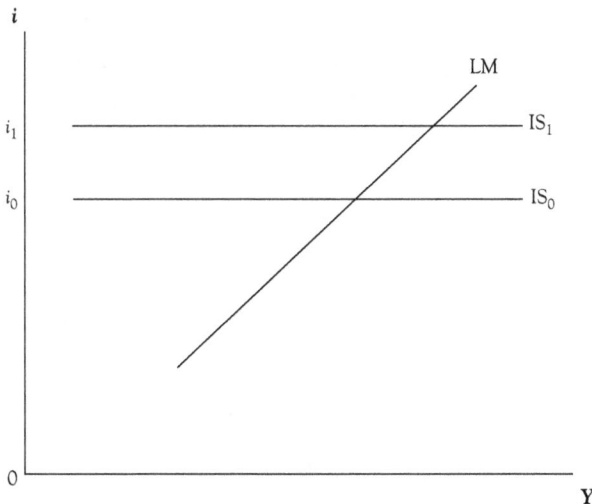

Figure 3.8. Horizontal IS and maximum effectiveness of monetary policy.

During recessionary periods it is better to have the MPC = 1 because it will increase the effectiveness of the multiplier effect and there is ample excess capacity, allowing for zero new investment. However, people are reluctant to increase their expenditures, let alone to have zero savings. Of course, the unemployed have no choice but to curtail their consumption due to lack of income.

Vertical IS

One requirement for a liquidity trap is that the interest elasticity of invest-ment be low. At the extreme, this means that investment is completely inelastic with respect to the interest rate, which makes the IS curve verti-cal. The existence of a vertical IS curve is difficult to fathom. For the IS schedule to be vertical it is necessary that the investment function to be horizontal. A horizontal investment function implies that the marginal propensity to invest is infinite, which requires the MPC to be zero. Under this scenario, any additional income is saved and none consumed. A zero MPC implies that consumers are at their respective saturation points and do not desire to consume any more when their income increases. If this is the case it is not clear why consumers might wish to invest, which

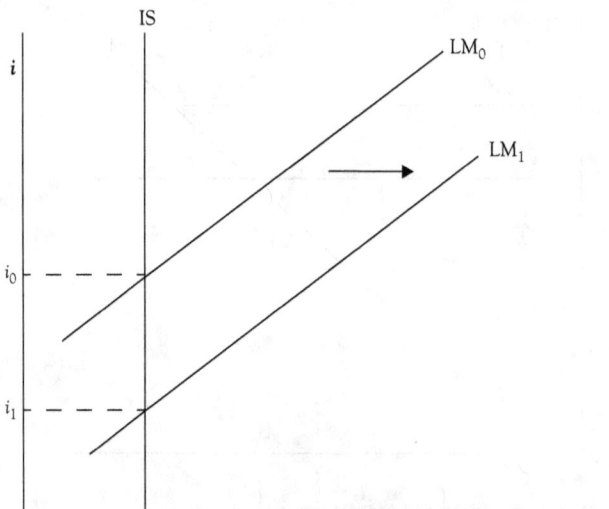

Figure 3.9. Vertical IS and ineffectiveness of monetary policy.

provides additional income in the form of interest and additional output as a result of investment in new machinery. Both of these conclusions contradict the possibility of saturation point for all goods. It is possible that investment cannot increase due to the crowding out effect, which is at its maximum when the IS curve is vertical, as in Figure 3.9. Under these conditions an expansionary fiscal policy can only increase the interest rate without increasing investment or output.

SECTION II

Interest Rate and Fiscal Theory

CHAPTER 4

The Role of Interest Rate in Fiscal Policy

It is believed that present consumption is preferred to future consumption. Parting with one's money deprives consumers from present-time consumption. The interest rate is compensation for the loss of immediate gratification. Different people place different values on this loss. Therefore, while some might be willing to lend or borrow at a given interest rate, others might not. This discrepancy is part of the reason for the existence of loanable funds. Lenders give up the use of their assets, and the utility that is derived from those assets, in return for earning income in the form of interest.

According to classical economists, who view the loanable funds market the same as any other good, the supply and demand for loanable funds determines the market's equilibrium interest rate. This static and partial equilibrium approach does not explain why funds are borrowed or lent. Chapter 3 provided a link between the interest rate and investment, which was used in the derivation of the IS schedule. There is also a link between the demand for money and the interest rate, which is used to obtain the LM schedule. The LM schedule is the loci of combinations of interest rates and incomes that result in equilibrium in the money market. It is worthwhile to repeat that lending money is not considered investment, while purchases of machinery and construction of new factory buildings are. In economics, whether a firm or an individual owns capital to invest is irrelevant. What is relevant is that funds can be used for investment or lent to others. The decision to lend or invest depends on the rate of return on the investment. When a firm can yield a return higher than other firms it will increase its investment by either using its own funds or by borrowing. However, when another firm can provide a higher return on investment the owner of funds can lend the money instead of investing it. In other words, funds will flow to investments with the highest returns.

This process will continue until the return to investment is the same as the interest rate.[1] Therefore, it is irrelevant who owns the capital when the loanable funds market is perfectly competitive.

Customarily, investment expenditures are made across relatively short periods of time, and the entire supply of investment funds is spent before any return is realized. The return to investment is periodic and therefore realized over an extended period, usually in different magnitudes. The stream of future returns or "prospective yields," according to Keynes, must be converted to their present value equivalent to be able to calculate their internal rate of return. This rate is compared with the market interest rate. Any investment with an internal rate of return higher than the market interest rate is an acceptable investment.

Definition

The **present value of future revenue** is the amount of money, if lent at the current interest rate, that would result in the same amount of revenue in the future as the income that was targeted.

Definition

The **internal rate of return** of an investment is the rate of interest that would equate the discounted present value of expected future yields to the cost of investment.

Interest Rate and Investment

The above discussion is similar to the views of classical economists. Keynes also accepts this relationship between interest rate and investment. Keynes refers to the rate of interest that is equal to the discounted present value of expected income from capital investment as the marginal efficiency of capital (MEC).[2]

Definition

Marginal efficiency of capital is the discount rate that would make the present value of a series of income from investment during its life equal to its supply price.

Recall that the return to capital occurs over a period of time and usually the amounts are different in each period. Keynes uses annuities to simplify the discussion.

Definition

An **annuity** is a financial product with fixed stream of payments over time.

Investors use the MEC to decide which investment is worthwhile based on the expected stream of future incomes. MEC pertains to the expectations of the future and is not the current yield of capital. Interest rates, however, are a current phenomenon. The future influences the present through the MEC, which helps determine the price for durable goods and its demand. As more capital goods are used for investment, the productivity of capital decreases, thus reducing the MEC. However, at the same time, an increase in the use of capital raises its price, that is, the interest rate. The process continues until the interest rate becomes equal to the MEC. Marshall uses a similar term with similar meaning, called **marginal net efficiency**, an observation made by Keynes.[3,4] The MEC explanation of investment clearly links it to the interest rate based on the expected stream of future earnings. On the other hand, there are alternative investment theories that do not establish any link between the interest rate and investment.

Accelerated Theory of Investment

According to the accelerated theory of investment the current level of output depends on a particular stock of capital and is a fraction of it.

$$x = \frac{K_t}{Y_t} \tag{4.1}$$

where K_t is the stock of capital in year t and Y_t is the output in the same year. Variable x is the fixed ratio of the two. The equation can be written as

$$K_t = xY_t \tag{4.2}$$

The constancy of x implies that equation 4.2 is true for the previous period as well.

$$K_{t-1} = xY_{t-1} \tag{4.3}$$

Subtracting equation 4.3 from equation 4.2 and rearranging the variables results in

$$K_t - K_{t-1} = x(Y_t - Y_{t-1}) = I_t - D_t \tag{4.4}$$

Equation 4.4 states that net investment is a multiple of change in output between two adjacent periods. On the other hand, net investment is the difference between gross investment (I_t) and depreciation (D_t). The term x is called the **accelerator coefficient**.

Definition

Accelerator coefficient is the magnitude of increase in investment due to a given increase in output/demand.

Under the accelerator theory of investment the determining factor for investment is output/demand and not the interest rate. The problem is that the theory only explains net investment, while aggregate demand depends on gross investment. The basic form presented here indicates that discrepancies in expected levels of investment are corrected in one period, which is an unrealistic assumption. The main feature of the theory, namely that the ratio of capital to output is constant, implies it is impossible to substitute labor for capital to meet the need for increased demand. This is unrealistic since labor can work overtime. Another issue with the theory is that it does not address the possibility of the existence of excess capacity, which is the same as eliminating the possibility of a recession. Finally, the theory assumes that firms would increase investment in response to an increase in demand, regardless of whether the firms expect the demand to continue to increase or not. However, all of these issues have been addressed in the modified versions of the theory. A common formulation explains gross investment I_t as:

$$I_t = \lambda(K_t^* - K_{t-1}) + \delta K_{t-1} \qquad 0 < \lambda, \delta < 1 \qquad (4.5)$$

where the asterisk indicates the desired level of capital stock. Other theories of investment include the internal funds theory and the neoclassical theory. In the case of the latter, the price of capital relative to the price of output, as well as the output level, determines the desired level of capital. The price of capital services is a function of the interest rate, the price of capital goods, and the tax rate on investment. Therefore, the interest rate is centrally important. Changes in government expenditures and taxes affect aggregate demand, and thus, output. This relationship between the interest rate and output is the foundation of the IS schedule.

Recall from Chapter 3 that the interest rate inversely affects the output. An increase in the interest rate reduces output, while a decrease in it raises output. This relationship reduces the impact of any expansionary stimulus because of the crowding out effect. In Chapter 3, we also saw that the extent of the crowding out effect depends on the magnitude of the multiplier effect. This magnitude is a function of the MPC and tax rate, which determines the slope of the IS schedule.

Crowding out also occurs when the government uses deficit financing to fund part of its expenditures. With an increase in national debt the interest rate appreciates due to increased demand for loanable funds. However, although the national debt of the United States in 2013 is at a record high, the nominal interest rate is at a historically low level. Combined with almost non-existing inflation the real interest rate is also low. This lack of crowding out could be due to several factors such as an easy money policy pursued by the Fed, a recession, or a lack of confidence in the future stemming from a lack of demand or uncertainty.

An expansionary fiscal policy would result in a higher equilibrium level of income as well as a higher interest rate. An expansionary monetary policy would result in higher equilibrium level of income and a lower equilibrium level of interest rate. This demonstrates that there is a major difference between fiscal and monetary policy with regard to interest rate outcomes. After the recession of 2008 in the United States, both income levels and interest rates have been low. Either monetary or fiscal expansion, or both, can be used to increase output and reduce unemployment.

However, due to public sentiment toward national debt and the stance of many politicians on taxes and expenditures, fiscal expansion is not taking place, at least not at a fast-enough pace. Fiscal expansion can take place either by increasing government expenditures or reducing taxes. Although the latter is popular with the public and politicians, a tax cut without a corresponding reduction in government expenditures will increase the national debt. Chapter 3 shows that a balanced budget multiplier will result in increased output, albeit much smaller than the increase through deficit financing. Consequently, a balanced budget reduction in taxes is contractionary. This is to say, a tax cut matched with an equal decrease in government expenditures will result in a decline in GDP, which is not a desirable outcome under any condition, let alone in the presence of an unemployment rate that is barely under 8%. Monetary expansion would have worked if it was not for the low interest rate, which might have been due to the presence of liquidity trap.

Each fiscal policy choice has different effects. An increase in government expenditures increases both G and C, while a reduction in taxes increases C. When a tax cut is combined with a reduction in government expenditures the effect of an increase in C is offset by a reduction in G. Since the marginal propensity to consume (spend) for the government is one, while that of the public is believed to be less than one, the net consequence is a reduction in output. The argument that an increase in consumption would result in an increase in investment cannot be substantiated because of a decline in government expenditures as well as the existence of excess production capacity. However, if government debt were to decrease the interest rate would fall due to a weakening of the crowding out effect. However, this statement is true only when the economy is not in a liquidity trap.

Expansionary fiscal policies include increases in government expenditures, decreases in taxes, or increases in investment subsidies. Unless an expansionary fiscal policy, regardless of its origin, is accompanied by an expansionary monetary policy, the result will be an increase in the interest rate. The first two options cause an increase in the interest rate through a shift in aggregate expenditures while the last option will increase the demand for investment, and hence its price, directly. Therefore, when expansionary fiscal policy consists of increased government expenditures or tax cuts it is important to combine it with an easy monetary policy to avoid crowding out and causing a reduction in investment, which will offset part of the expansionary fiscal policy.

Figure 4.1 depicts a situation in which the economy is not at the full-employment output level of Y^*. Although the graph provides a point where the IS and LM curve intersect (E) the point does not correspond to the full-employment level. The output level corresponding to any point such as E, A, B, or C can be improved by either shifting IS_0 to IS_1 or shifting the LM_0 to LM_1 to stimulate the economy. The resulting equilibrium points of E_1 and E_2 correspond to full employment. The fiscal stimulus, that is the shift in IS, increases the interest rate to i_2 that corresponds to E_2, while the monetary stimulus, that is the shift in LM, decreases the interest rate to i_1, corresponding to E_1. Equilibrium points E_1 and E_2 represent the final resting point of each expansionary policy after all the endogenous responses and reactions to one or the other approach are completed, and the full-employment level of output has been achieved. However, the impact on economic agents is very different depending on which policy is implemented. An expansionary policy resulting in a lower interest rate benefits investors, while increased government expenditures helps the constituents that receive the expenditures. Defense expenditures help the defense industry, while

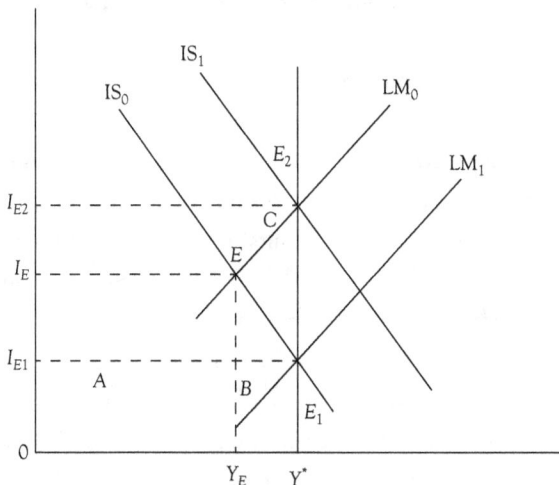

Figure 4.1. Full employment output through fiscal or monetary policy.

a meal program for the poor or elderly assists the recipients. However, a tax reduction can benefit everybody, regardless of their income, except for those that are exempt from paying taxes. Since the United States has a progressive tax system, a fixed percent reduction in everybody's taxes affects the poor less than the rich.

Since the beneficiaries of these policies are different, and potentially each group can gain substantially from a common goal of national full employment, each group would exert its own influence, be it through voting politicians into or out of the office, exertion of political pressure through special interest lobbies, or behaving corruptly.

The above discussion of achieving full employment through expansionary fiscal or monetary policy is based purely on economic theory and political economy. Economic theory alone cannot determine which policy will endure or which group will succeed in guiding the government through the path that is most beneficial to its constituents. This discussion also sidesteps the dispute between fiscal and monetary advocates. Each group claims that the policy of the other group is ineffective or less efficient. By the term efficiency we refer to the speed of achieving the desired full employment level of output. This discussion also ignores the ongoing dispute regarding the ability to implement one policy or the other, the accuracy in timing expansionary policy, or difficulty in estimating the appropriate amount of expansion required to achieve the desired objective. Some of these issues were discussed in Chapter 2 under the topic of inside and outside lags.

An important distinction between the classical and Keynesian economists is how the interest rate is determined. According to classical economic theory the interest rate is determined through decisions to save and invest. In fact, investment for these economists is a kind of consumption. An increase in investment goods results in an increase in the production of consumer goods in the future. Therefore, investment is a mechanism that shifts consumption from the present time to future via the influence of the interest rate. Keynesians, on the other hand, argue that the interest rate is determined in the money market. However, for them, the link between investment and the interest rate is through the MEC, which is based on the present value of the expected future stream of earnings from investment.

CHAPTER 5

Liquidity Preference

The notion of liquidity preference provides another way of conceptualizing the demand for money. However, the term money is a broader concept than liquidity. Money is a temporary abode of value,[1] and it can also be defined as anything that is acceptable in exchange for a good or service. For more detail on definitions of money and its different types refer to Naghshpour.[2] The distinction among the types of money is based on the ease of converting it to cash, or its liquidity. Therefore, the concept of liquidity preference is concerned with the demand for cash balances, or more precisely, the question of why people hold cash when other forms of money, such as a certificates of deposit, or assets, such as stocks and bonds, earn interest. The answer to this question is an integral part of the fiscal theory suggested by Keynes.

Keynes questions the notion that the interest rate is determined by the supply and demand for investment.[3] Classical economists believed that the interest rate is determined by the amount of savings on the supply side and by the marginal productivity of capital on the demand side. Under the classical approach, starting from an equilibrium point, assume the marginal productivity of capital increases because of a new invention, a new product, or a technological advance in the production of a good. In this scenario, the demand for investment increases and creates disequilibrium in the capital market. This increased demand results in an increase in the interest rate. Consequently, some investments become unprofitable while savings increase in response to the more lucrative interest rate.

In the classical analysis changes in supply of money do not affect the amount of savings or investment; therefore, the supply of money has no effect on interest rates.

Keynes argues that the interest rate is determined in the money market as a result of the interaction between the supply and demand for money. Keynes does not dispute that money is demanded for transaction purposes; however, he claims that money is also demanded for speculative motives, which is a function of the interest rate. Unlike classical economists who claim interest is the reward for postponing consumption, Keynes believes that interest is the price of giving up liquidity. Differences in expectations about future interest rates and uncertainty about financial assets affect the demand for money for speculative motives. It is noteworthy that Keynes does not dispute the importance of the marginal productivity of capital in decisions regarding investment. In fact, his analysis uses the concept of the marginal efficiency of capital developed by Marshall.[4] However, while notions such as the marginal product of capital and the marginal efficiency of capital are calculable, Keynes's use of investors' level of confidence as a determinant of speculative demand for money is not. The idea that money is demanded for three different motives and each is a function of different factors might be acceptable theoretically, but in practice it is doubtful that people divide their money into three parts and keep them separate to meet the demand for each of these different motives.

The demand for money based on the speculative motive depends on the uncertainty of the future. Keynes hypothesizes that it is possible to have a demand for money that is perfectly elastic with respect to the interest rate. This possibility does not necessarily imply that the situation should be everlasting or that the demand for speculative money has to always be flat. However, it does imply that as long as a segment of the demand curve is flat the economy will be in a liquidity trap, meaning that regardless of the increase in the magnitude of the supply of money, the demand for it is not satiated.

It can be shown that classical economists' predictions of the outcome of monetary policy represent a special case of Keynesian theory. According to Keynes, the special case happens to differ substantially from the economic reality of 1928 and the Great Depression. Monetary policy became ineffective during the Great Depression because the demand for money was not satisfied in spite of the increase in supply. Changes in the supply of money do not affect the interest rate when the economy is in a liquidity trap. Keynes's solution to this shortcoming is direct intervention by the government through fiscal policy. An expansionary fiscal policy can be achieved via an increase in government expenditures, a decrease in taxes, or both. Any of these actions indicate that government expenditures will exceed its revenue, which means that for the duration of the policy and possibly shortly after, there will be deficit financing. When a government has a surplus it can accomplish expansionary fiscal policy by reducing or eliminating the surplus. However, when there is little or no surplus during a recession the result of deficit financing is a mounting deficit.

One possible consequence of increasing national debt is the crowding out effect, as explained in Chapter 3. It is important to realize that the above discussion is based on the notion of *ceteris paribus*, or other things being equal. For example, the state of technology is assumed to remain constant and no external shock, positive or negative, is allowed. These assumptions also apply to monetary authorities' behavior. It is possible to counteract and offset the effect of an expansionary fiscal policy with a contractionary monetary policy.

Therefore, in order for the above discussion to be valid, it is necessary for the monetary policy to either remain constant or to be expansionary. The latter case is the preferred option as the government and the citizens wish to end recession and unemployment sooner rather than later. In fact, Keynes emphasizes this point: "The State will have to exercise a guiding influence on the propensity to consume partly through its scheme of taxation, partly by fixing the rate of interest, and partly, perhaps, in other ways."[5] It is important to keep in mind that a major problem, according to Keynes, is the instability of investment expenditures, which is caused by uncertainty, speculation, and risk, especially during recessionary periods. The acceptance of Keynes' policy recommendations resulted in increases in the size of government. The increased government role in the economy was also a consequence of demand for social justice and a reduction in income inequality. The increase in the size and power of governments is also, in part, a response to the increase in the power of large corporations, which sometimes have annual incomes that exceed the GDP of a large proportion of the world's countries, even developed ones.

A major contribution of Keynes is that he shows that decentralized economies may not result in equilibrium prices, which clear the market. This is a direct challenge to Walrasian equilibrium theory in which all prices are settled correctly and instantly through the silent auctioneer.

The market's inability to clear all prices under this scenario indicates that unemployment is a possibility in market economies. The attack on the Walrasian approach was continued by Clower[6] and later by neo-Keynesians such as Barro and Grossman[7] and Malinvaud.[8] The neo-Keynesian views are discussed in Chapter 8.

Liquidity Trap

In Keynesian economics the interest rate is determined in the money market based on the supply and demand for money. The supply of money is assumed to be exogenously determined by the monetary authorities, at least in the simplest of the scenarios. It would be unrealistic to believe that monetary authorities arbitrarily or capriciously determine the amount of money supply in the economy. However, it is not unrealistic to assume that in the short run the supply of money does not respond to changes in the market. This is due to an inside lag and also the inability to distinguish between random fluctuations and trends in the demand for money in the short run. Of the transaction, speculative, and precautionary motives affecting the demand for money, only speculative demand is believed to be a function of the interest rate.

The agreed relationship between speculative demand for money and the interest rate is an inverse relationship. At higher rates of interest the demand for money is less than when the interest rate is low. Another relevant factor is expectations about the future of interest rates. When the interest rate is low more people would expect it to increase than when it is high. This heightened expectation by a larger group of economic agents increases the demand for speculative money. At least theoretically, it is possible that at low enough interest rates, the demand for money becomes perfectly elastic, that is horizontal, thus increasing speculative demand to an infinitely high level. Under this scenario, attempts to lower the interest rate by increasing the supply of money will fail because of an insatiable demand for money. Keynes does not provide an example of a period in which a liquidity trap exists. His focus instead is on demonstrating its possibility and offering a solution to solve the unemployment problem of the Great Depression. Earlier works on this topic include Tobin,[9] Fellner,[10] Meltzer,[11] and Ando and Modigliani.[12] More recent works include Hanes,[13] Pollin,[14] and Ueda.[15]

The effectiveness of monetary policy, according to Keynes, depends on the responsiveness of interest rates to changes in the money supply, the responsiveness of investment to changes in the interest rate, and the magnitude of the multiplier. A liquidity trap is the extreme case of the lack of responsiveness of the interest rate to changes in the supply of money. Even if the extreme case of a liquidity trap does not exist, high expectations of an increase in the interest rate in the future can increase the speculative demand for money, thus reducing the responsiveness of the interest rate to expansionary monetary policy. However, it is not necessary for the extreme case to prevail to make monetary policy (relatively) ineffective. The responsiveness of investment to changes in the interest rate is as important as the responsiveness of the interest rate to changes in the supply of money. For example, idle capacity exists during recessions, and therefore it does not make sense to increase investment simply because the interest rate has decreased as a result of expansionary monetary policy.

Liquidity Trap and Unemployment

A key component of Keynesian analysis is the downward rigidity of wages and prices. This situation can be compared to a ratchet mechanism that operates similar to an automobile jack. The effect of liquidity trap can be traced to unemployment. First, using Figure 5.1 track the effect of a monetary expansion policy. Start from an initial position of equilibrium, where all the pertinent points are marked with a subscript zero. An expansionary monetary policy shifts the LM schedule to the right. There is no longer equilibrium at point E_0 and all the new positions are marked with subscript one. As explained in Chapter 3, a point on the IS schedule indicates an equilibrium point in the goods market and a point on the LM schedule represents an equilibrium point in the money market. Therefore, at both points E_0 and E_1, the goods market and the money market are at equilibrium.

Panel A depicts a typical IS-LM interaction that results in equilibrium in both the money and the goods market. Panel B uses the 45 degree line to transfer changes in income to the labor market in Panel C, where the relationship between labor and output is presented in a typical production function. Panel D links the supply of and demand for labor to

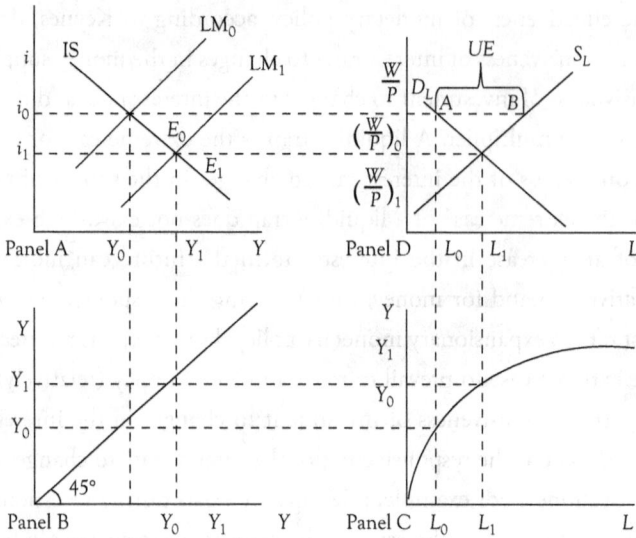

Figure 5.1. **IS-LM in the case of labor market disequilibrium.**

real wages. The equilibrium point E_0 is not necessarily a desirable position. Tracing the output level Y_0 to Panel B provides the necessary link to obtain the amount of labor necessary to produce that level of output, which is marked as Y_0. Connecting the line stemming from labor level L_0 and the equilibrium point L_0 provides point A in Panel D on the demand line, which corresponds to the real wage rate of W_0/P_0. At this level of real wages the supply of labor, marked by point B, exceeds the demand for labor. Therefore, an excess supply of labor exists, which is known customarily as unemployment.

Definition

Unemployment refers to an economic condition in which there are people who are actively seeking employment at the prevailing market wage but cannot find a job.

Note that under normal conditions, without the presence of liquidity trap, a market economy is fully capable of having disequilibrium in the labor market while the goods and money markets are at equilibrium. This can happen only under the condition of sticky wages, when nominal wages do not decline due to resistance from workers. Some, if not all, unemployed workers refuse to accept lower nominal wages. Some argue that unemployment compensations and other social welfare programs prolong unemployment by reducing the need to be employed. This claim has not been tested scientifically. Regardless, these safety nets did not contribute to the length of the Great Depression because they did not exist then.

The outcome of analysis would be different under the classical assumption of wage and price adjustments. Under classical assumptions an excess supply of labor exerts downward pressure on nominal wages. A decline in wages decreases the cost, and thus the price of goods. Both nominal and real wages decline until the real wage becomes $(W/P)_1$. At this real wage the labor market is at equilibrium. Lower prices increase the real value of the money and result in a real increase in the supply of money. The full-employment equilibrium corresponds to higher output level of Y_1 in Panel C. Using the transition quadrant B, output Y_1 is connected to the IS schedule at point E_1. The new equilibrium is obtained by a shift in the LM schedule to the right, which reflects an increase in the supply of money to meet the increased demand for money, which is necessitated by the increased output/income. When the real value of money increases the excess money in the economy causes a reduction in the interest rate, which in turn increases investment. Aggregate demand increases, which offsets part of the price decrease. The final outcome is that all markets, including the labor market, are at equilibrium.

The presence of a liquidity trap means that at least a portion of the LM schedule is flat and the demand for money is perfectly elastic with regard to interest rate. Figure 5.2 depicts the case similar to that of Figure 5.1 where the money and goods markets are at equilibrium at point E_0 while the labor market experiences unemployment. The initial levels of output, labor, and real wages are the same as in Figure 5.1 and are marked by subscript zero.

Once again notice that real wages are higher than the market clearing level and there is unemployment in the market. Following the classical economists, assume prices and wages are not sticky and can adjust downward. Unemployment forces nominal wages to decline, which reduces real wages. Reduction in wages reduces production costs and hence prices. Consequently, the real supply of money increases and shifts LM_0 to LM_1. However, because of the liquidity trap, the interest rate does not decline,

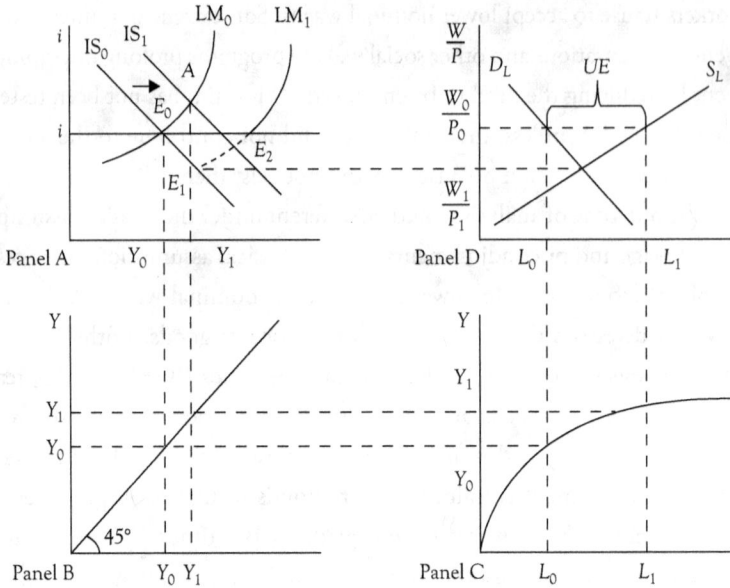

Figure 5.2. Unemployment with equilibrium in IS-LM schedule.

and the entire increase in the supply of money is absorbed by speculative demand for money. The equilibrium point for the money market is at point A, which is on the LM curve but not on the IS curve; therefore, the goods market is not at equilibrium. In order for the goods market to be at equilibrium at the full employment level the interest rate must fall to i_1 and the equilibrium point is reached at E_2. Although at point E_2 the goods market is at equilibrium, the money market is not. Point E_2 is a hypothetical equilibrium point since the interest rate cannot fall in the scenario above because of the presence of a liquidity trap. Consequently, investment cannot increase and aggregate demand remains the same, which is less than the amount necessary to match the full employment output. Therefore, unlike the classical case with flexible price and wage adjustments, prices will decline proportionately to wages while the real wage remains at the original level, that is,

$$\frac{W_0}{P_0} = \frac{W_1}{P_1}$$

At the original real wage level the excess in the labor market cannot be resolved and the market economy fails to eliminate unemployment, contrary to the claim of classical economists.

Earlier, it was pointed out that a factor that affects this outcome is the elasticity of investment with regard to the interest rate. It is not difficult to show that when there is no liquidity trap, but investment is inelastic with respect to the interest rate, the market economy will fail to create a general equilibrium as well.

CHAPTER 6

Operation and Effectiveness of Fiscal Policy

Fiscal policy represents government intervention in the economy through changes in government expenditures and taxes. The presumption is fiduciary conduct by the government. For example, expenditures on infrastructure or national defense are believed to be conducted in the most efficient and reasonable way. Government contracts are required to have multiple bids and the bids are examined for specifications and costs. This does not mean government employees do not make mistakes or that nothing fails in practice. Rather, the assumption means that there is no reason for deliberate inefficiency or sabotage.

Nevertheless, ineptness, lack of information, or even human greed and self-indulgence could cause inefficiency in government procurements.

Changes in aggregate demand are affected by changes in consumption, investment, government expenditures, and net trade. Consumption expenditures are believed to maximize the utility of individuals. Investment expenditures are believed to be made rationally and for the purpose of profit maximization. At least in the case of investment, there is evidence that not all investments are successful, and therefore may not be "wise or prudent;" although undoubtedly entrepreneurs of failed investments took every precaution and analyzed the market before engaging in the investment, and thus "acted wisely." For investments that are financed, lenders require submission of a sound business plan and cost–benefit analysis. Government expenditures are believed to be "wise" in this sense as well. At least in theory, elected officials who misuse public funds in an electoral system can be voted out of office, or even impeached. There are also stringent laws for abuse of government funds by employees and elected officials. However, the safeguards against abuse of public funds do not play a major role in and are not important for the outcome of fiscal policy, since aggregate income is affected by changes in government expenditures, wise or otherwise.

Increases in government expenditures are expansionary while increases in taxes are contractionary. Although true, this statement is overly simplistic. It fails to address how the government increases its expenditures in the first place, or what the government does with its increased tax revenues. One logical response that answers both concerns is that increased government expenditures are generated through increased taxes. The effect of this balanced-budget expansionary fiscal policy was discussed in Chapter 3. An increase in government expenditures increases output and income, which in turn increases tax revenues. On the other hand, an increase in taxes reduces consumption and investment expenditures, which reduces income and consequently government tax revenues. A more realistic model must account for all the variables that are actually affected by other factors in the economy. For example, taxes are affected by income levels, which in turn are affected by the level of unemployment, and investment is a function of interest rate. All of these variables, as well as consumption and government expenditures, affect equilibrium in the IS and/or LM schedule. In the case of an open economy with trade, net exports also affect the factors of the model. In equation 3.13 (Chapter 3), it was shown that the multiplier effect in the presence of a flat tax rate of t percent is equal to:

$$k = \frac{1}{1 - c(1 - t)}$$

The factors that change the multiplier cause changes in the slope of IS curve. An increase in MPC, for example, reduces the denominator, which increases the multiplier effect. A larger MPC implies a greater increase in aggregate demand, which translates into a smaller slope for IS curve, or a flatter line. An increase in the tax rate decreases the denominator of the multiplier, which makes the multiplier smaller. Therefore, the corresponding IS curve becomes steeper. Since the IS curve is based on the relationship between the interest rate and output through changes in investment, the greater the responsiveness of investment to the interest rate, the steeper the IS curve. Note that the above simplified multiplier does not include an interest rate. Equation 3.10 incorporates the interest rate by substituting it for the investment function. For any LM curve with a given slope, the flatter the IS curve the greater the impact of a shift in the IS curve; therefore, the greater the impact of fiscal policy. The extreme cases of horizontal IS and vertical LM were discussed in Chapter 3. These extreme cases exemplify, respectively, the most and least effective cases of fiscal and monetary policy combinations.

Some Pertinent Issues

Fiscal policy can be implemented through changes in government expenditures and taxes. Changes in taxes can be implemented in several ways. Different types of taxes at local, state, and federal levels consist of excise, sales, property, and income, to name a few. Taxes can set at a fixed amount, such as an import tax per item, regardless of its value or the income of the importer; proportionate, such as sales tax; based on value, such as property tax; or multirate, such as income tax. Taxes that are not a function of income cause shifts in aggregate demand while taxes that are a function of income have ripple effects in the economy. This is because taxes accrue with each round of change in income that is generated from changes in fiscal policy. Taxes that affect the wealthy, such as property taxes, also affect aggregate demand, for two reasons. First, they affect income because of tax payments. Second, they affect wealth; therefore, they have an inverse effect on consumption. A property tax increase reduces wealth, and thus, reduces consumption because of a wealth effect. For a given level of income, a wealthier person will have greater consumption than someone with less wealth. For simplicity, typical IS curves are created based on a flat rate tax system. The type of tax and its formation, for example progressive taxes, affects the degree to which people at various income levels bear the tax burden. For example, a tax levied on the consumption of cigarettes affects both smokers and cigarette producers based on the price elasticity of demand for cigarettes.

Government expenditures can be in the form of consumption, such as the purchase of an automobile for official use; investment, such as building a plant to produce nuclear missiles; or, for the purpose of social welfare, such as transfer payments. Some government expenditures are welcome in general, such as the establishment of national defense, while others create more debate, such as transfer payments. The amount of investment by the United States government has been declining since the 1970s and is currently averaging less than 1.5% of the GDP of the country. An increase in government expenditure is expansionary and stimulates the economy regardless of its form or purpose, while an increase in taxes is contractionary regardless of its form or purpose.

An expansionary fiscal policy, in the form of increased government expenditures or decreased taxes, shifts aggregate expenditures upward causing an upward shift in IS curve. Assuming there is an idle capacity in the economy and that an accommodative monetary policy is in place, the result is an increase in aggregate output until the full employment level of output is restored, and the idle capacity of firms is used up. Idle capacity means there is unemployment in the labor and capital markets. An accommodating monetary policy means that the supply of money is increased, rather than kept constant or decreased.

Pigou Effect

Pigou might be considered the last relevant classical economist. Pigou argues that in cases where prices and wages are not rigid downward the Keynesian model would result in full employment equilibrium.[1] This is in contrast to Keynes's claim of equilibrium with persistent unemployment because, as Pigou points out, Keynes ignored the wealth effect. The following discussion utilizes Figure 5.2, which was used earlier to discuss the liquidity trap in Chapters 3 and 5. Assume, as Keynes does, that the goods market and the money market are at equilibrium; the points on the graph designated by subscript zero. Again, due to excess supply of labor wages will decline and as a result prices will fall.

Pigou points out that a reduction in prices increases wealth.[2] The consequence of increased wealth is an increase in expenditure, which shifts the IS curve to the right to IS_1, in addition to shifting the LM curve to the right due to the decrease in prices. Pigou argues that the wealth effect is sufficient to increase aggregate demand to the full employment level, thus eliminating the possibility of equilibrium in goods and money markets while persistent unemployment remains, as Keynes claims can occur. Therefore, wage and price rigidity are necessary for the existence of equilibrium in the goods and money markets but unemployment in the labor market might be at less than full employment. Pigou's views on these matters were then changed and modified over time.

Tobin questions the inevitability of full employment output as a result of the wealth effect.[3] In fact, expectations of further price declines might induce consumers to postpone consumption, and thus, reduce aggregate consumption, which would raise unemployment rather than reducing it. A similar outcome can arise if firms expect a continued recession, which would induce them to postpone new investment. Of course, different possible combinations of the expectations by these two groups can cast doubts on the inevitability of full employment equilibrium. In 1933, Fisher pointed out that an increase in bankruptcies would result in a decline of economic conditions and increased unemployment. The consequences of these possibilities imply a stronger case for the effectiveness of a fiscal policy.

Banks accept deposits from the public that is they borrow, and lend their money to firms and individuals for investment and consumption. The result is creation of new money.[4] Students of introductory economics and the general public find this analysis a little uncomfortable, because it does not take into account that the money created by bank lending also constitutes a liability for their borrowers. Therefore, although the wealth of banks increases because of the additional money, their liabilities also increase by the same amount resulting in zero net wealth. It seems that somehow there should be a distinction between currency, in the form of cash and deposit, and the money created by lending existing money, and that the latter should be treated differently than freshly minted money. The money created in the private sector is called inside money, while the money created by cash notes, coins, and bank reserves is called outside money. Another way of expressing these concepts is to realize that outside money is the money injected into the private sector as a transfer, or as a result of a transaction in goods market, while inside money originates from monetary transactions, such as an exchange of assets. The distinction is that outside money represents net wealth while inside money represents gross wealth. To convert money into net wealth they must first subtract the amount of their liabilities. The result is a substantial decline in the wealth effect.

Pesek and Saving and Johnson disagree with the notion that inside money is not net wealth.[5,6] A related issue is the matter of government bonds. When people acquire government bonds their wealth increases. However, because government bonds increase national debt, public wealth declines in the long run when the bond has to be paid by taxes. Although a decline in prices makes bonds more valuable, the subsequent increase in additional taxes offsets the wealth effect. Even Pigou expressed doubt about the significance of the magnitude of the wealth effect in real life.[7]

Automatic Stabilizers

During expansionary periods, incomes increase because more people work and also prices and wages increase. Consequently, taxes increase as well. Under a progressive tax system, tax rates increase substantially as nominal income levels increase. As the economy approaches full employment, the danger of inflation increases and it becomes necessary to slow the economy's expansion through anti-inflationary measures. Since a progressive tax code is in effect, the increase in taxes operates as an automatic stabilizer to slow the expansion. This argument is valid only if the government does not spend the additional tax revenue. If it does, this will accelerate the economic expansion as shown in Chapter 3 when discussing the balanced budget multiplier.

Taxes existed well before the idea of discretionary fiscal and monetary policies were formed. Since the expansion of social safety nets in the 20th century, the magnitude and role of automatic stabilizers have increased. Welfare programs are designed to help people with low or no income to attain higher living standards. During expansionary periods, the number of people that qualify to receive transfer payments decreases as more people work and incomes increase. The purpose of automatic stabilizers is to soften the magnitude of economic peaks and troughs. As income of individuals and the profits of firms increase during an expansionary period, the amount of taxes and the tax rates also increase, thus weakening the expansionary effects on incomes and profits. The opposite occurs during economic downturns and recessions. As incomes and profits decline, less tax and lower rates apply, therefore aggregate demand does not decrease as much.

In addition to the incidental effect of taxes as automatic stabilizers, there are numerous other automatic stabilizers that have been established, such as unemployment insurance, which softens the negative impact of recessions on individuals. Every employer and employee pays a portion of a worker's wage or salary toward the unemployment benefit. This tax is antiexpansionary or reduces aggregate demand during booms and is anticontractionary during economic downturns. When a worker is laid off because of an economic downturn, he receives a fraction of his income for a period of time. The amount and duration of payments depends on workers' length of employment and income. This payment is anticontractionary and reduces the magnitude and duration of economic downturns.

Neither charity nor the role of government in providing charity is new. The only thing new is the understanding of dampening effect on the business cycle. Ironically, during expansionary times more people can afford being charitable but less people need it, while during contractionary periods less people can afford being charitable but more people need it. Situations like this warrant government intervention by extracting funds from the economy during expansionary periods and injecting them into the economy during contractionary periods. Recent history has shown that most governments spend the additional revenues generated during expansionary periods through automatic stabilizers. Therefore, during contractionary periods, funds are not available to slow the economic downturn and the government has to resort to deficit financing. However, accumulating debt has serious economic consequences, such as the crowding out of investment. Another consequence of large budget deficits is the possibility of hyperinflation. Increases in the money supply cause hyperinflations, and most if not all historical cases of hyperinflation have occurred in countries with large budget deficits. Since automatic stabilizers reduce aggregate expenditures during expansionary periods and increase them during contractionary periods, they reduce the multiplier effect during the former and increase the multiplier effect during the latter.

Effectiveness of Automatic Stabilizers

The effectiveness of automatic stabilizers stems from the fact that their inside lag is zero. As soon as income increases taxes increase, and when one is unemployed he or she can collect the benefit without need for any legislative or administrative decision. The outside lag should also be zero as the process is automatic and instantaneous. However, it is doubtful that automatic stabilizers could eliminate business cycles by themselves, thus necessitating discretionary fiscal and monetary intervention.

The effectiveness of automatic stabilizers depends on the responsiveness of employment and personal income to fiscal instruments, such as taxes, and government expenditures in the short run.[8] A negative side effect of automatic stabilizers during economic downturns is the increase in national debt, which exacerbates expectations of a future tax increase. This statement is only partially true, since it ignores the fact that during recoveries, government expenditures decrease due to the same automatic stabilizers while its revenues increase because of the increase in citizens' income and the existence of progressive taxing. Cassou and Lansing demonstrate "that stabilization policies can produce welfare levels that are nearly identical to those of welfare maximization policies and that both welfare maximization and stabilization policies yield large welfare gains and modest growth losses relative to growth maximization policies."[9] However, attempting to stabilize all macroeconomic variables together proves to be impossible, since stabilizing one variable increases the volatility of another macroeconomic variable. The effectiveness in reducing the length, frequency, and severity of recessions is demonstrated by Diebold and Rudebusch and Romer.[10,11] Other evidences in support of the effectiveness of automatic stabilizers are Christiano and Harrison and Cohen and Follette.[12,13]

CHAPTER 7

Questioning Keynesian Theory

The main shortcoming of the quantity theory manifested itself in its inability to avoid or soften the magnitude of the Great Depression. Here is not the place to determine whether it was the shortcoming of the theory, or the monetary authorities themselves, that failed. Keynes offers a plausible explanation of both types of shortcomings and suggests a potential solution.[1] Arguably, the greatest outcome of the Keynesian solution is the introduction of discretionary policy. Discretionary policy requires direct engagement of government in the economic affairs of the country with the intent to reduce the magnitude, or distance, between peak and troughs in businesses cycles and also reduce their duration. Discretionary fiscal policy dominated economic thinking and policy orientations in many countries between 1936 and the late 1960s. Serious challenges to Keynesian theory and its criticism of the quantity theory, as well as its solutions, have been made. For example, criticism of the wealth effect by Pigou is discussed in Chapter 6. Hammond provides a review of the advocates of fiscal and monetary economists on the subject of business cycles.[2]

New Classical School

Friedman revitalized the quantity theory and raised serious concerns about the Keynesian approach in general, and discretionary policy in particular.[3] A serious issue is the simplistic way of incorporating expectations into fiscal theory as compared to the treatment of expectations by Muth, and later by Lucas, who used the notion of rational expectations to demonstrate the theoretical neutrality of money.[4,5] Sargent's implementation of the rational expectations hypothesis into the subject of equilibrium analysis brought about the emergence of the "new classical" school.[6]

New classical economists revived the assumptions of price flexibility, instantaneous market clearance, and perfect competition. This is a hardline approach to classical economics and approaches macroeconomics from an equilibrium perspective. This approach is equivalent to a "fully specified general equilibrium microeconomics." If the notion is correct that the Keynesian approach is a revolution, then the work of Lucas is a counterrevolution.[7] The beginning of the new classical school can be traced to Lucas.[8] Unlike Keynes, advocates of the rational expectations hypothesis treat expectations as an endogenous variable.[9,10] Without doubt the foundations of issues concerning the new classical school and its conclusions are embedded in monetary theory, especially the quantity theory of Friedman. However, it is the rational expectations hypothesis component of the new classical approach that renders Keynesian models ineffective. That is not to say that the new classical approach of Lucas shares the same methodologies as the modern quantity theory espoused by monetarists like Friedman. In fact, in terms of their theoretical approaches Lucas follows Walras, while Friedman pursues Marshall.

The analytical approach of the new classical school is based on Walras's notion of general equilibrium and uses microeconomic foundations as the basis for forming macroeconomic theory; firms maximize profits, consumers maximize utility. Like the classical economists, they assume homoeconomicus is rational, but this rationality is explained as endogenous in the context of rational expectation hypothesis, which is the first time this approach is applied. The assumption of rationality excludes the possibility of a money illusion. Money illusion implies that if a currency's unit of denomination were to change, for example from dollars to cents, people would think they have greater income and wealth.

Definition

Money illusion indicates that economic agents make decisions based on nominal rather than real variables. This implies irrational patterns of behavior in response to changes in nominal terms.

The addition of price and wage flexibility revives the Walrasian instantaneous auctioneer; thus, the neutrality of money is assured, and real variables cannot be affected by nominal changes, as is implicit in the Phillips

Curve.[11] Thus, the new classical school accepts the possibility of imperfect information. Mankiw, Akerlof and Yellen, and Blanchard and Kiyotaki demonstrate that a small price rigidity under imperfect competition can cause proportionately much larger economic effects.[12-14]

Definition

Money is said to be **neutral** when changes in the stock of money affect only nominal, not real, variables.

Chapter 5 pointed out that the fiscal theory of Keynes distinguishes between uncertainty and risk. In the case of uncertainty, there is no probability distribution available to be used to provide insight about uncertainty. However, it is possible to calculate a probability for risk using an appropriate probability distribution function. The new classical model does not address uncertainty since business cycles are believed to have been drawn from an identical distribution function, which makes sense under the assumptions of the rational expectations hypothesis. These models are solely concerned with risk. The post-Keynesians (see Chapter 9) question this view and claim that uncertainty prevails in the real world, at least at the current level of statistical knowledge. Interestingly, the Austrian School objects to this and other aspects of rational expectations hypothesis.[15] One important methodological issue is that when the given expectations of a group are broken down by identifiable strata, the expectations of each stratum can be and often are different. It is not unrealistic to have variations in expectations about a particular economic phenomenon, for example future unemployment, because of differences in age, gender, race, ethnicity, current employment, income, wealth, and education, to name but few.

New classical economists return to Walras's instantaneous auctioneer idea by remarking that observed data, by default, represent equilibrium points. Consequently, they are assuming that the economy is always at equilibrium, both in the short run and in the long run, thus eliminating a point of contention between advocates of fiscal and monetary policy. The implications are that economic agents are optimizing their objectives and that the prevailing market structure is that of perfect competition. As a result, Pareto optimality prevails; hence, consumer surplus and producer surplus are maximized.

Definition

Consumer surplus is the sum of the differences between the market clearing price and the maximum price that each consumer is willing to pay.

Definition

Pareto optimal distribution is a distribution in which no one can be made better-off without making someone else worse-off.

Definition

Producer surplus is the sum of the differences between the market clearing price and the minimum price that each producer is willing to charge.

In the case of consumer surplus, consumers are willing and able to pay a price higher than the market price, but do not have to do so. In Figure 7.1 the areas above the price and below the demand curve represent consumer surplus. In the case of producer surplus, producers are willing and able to receive a price lower than the market clearing price, but they do not have to do so. In Figure 7.1 the areas under the price and above the supply curve represent producer surplus. The market price is

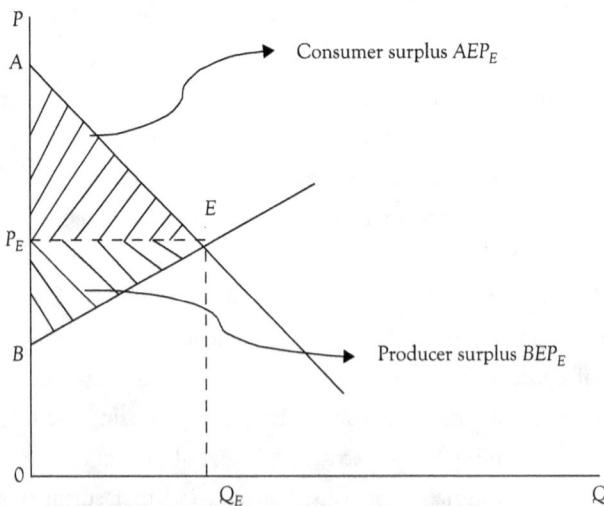

Figure 7.1. *Consumer and producer surpluses.*

determined by the least efficient and productive producer and the ability and willingness of the last consumer that can meet the market clearing price. Consumers with higher utility enjoy a consumer surplus, and more efficient producers reap a producer surplus.

Price adjustment in the new classical model is broader than in monetary theories, since the latter allows for disequilibrium in the short run, while the former does not. While the continuous equilibrium solves some of the problems of monetary theory and counters many of the main points of Keynesian theory, it also causes additional controversies. An implication of continuous equilibrium is that all unemployment is voluntary. In other words, the prevailing wages are the market-clearing wages and anyone who wishes to work at that wage is, in fact, actually working. However, this definition of unemployment is based on involuntary removal from work combined with the inability to find another job, while actively seeking one.

Another important element of the new classical models is the aggregate supply hypothesis. This hypothesis is based on the microeconomic foundations of the supply of labor in which each person has to decide on the amount of labor he is willing to supply versus the amount of leisure taken, at any given wage rate. An increase in real wages will induce more people to increase their supply of labor that is to reduce their leisure, as well as an increase in the number of people that participate in the labor market.

The microeconomic solution is obtained by utility maximization. Microeconomists utilize indifference curves to demonstrate how one's time is divided between leisure and labor. The sum of all individual labors determines the market labor supply. Depending on the magnitude of income and the substitution effect, as explained by Slutsky's equation, it is possible that as wages increase the supply of labor decreases, which creates a backward bending labor supply curve. It is also possible to have a forward falling supply curve where a decrease in real wages at the lower end of the wage spectrum could trigger an increase in the labor supply, due to an inability to sustain even a subsistence standard of living. In the more general case of an upward-sloping labor supply curve, current real wages are compared to expected real wages. When the former exceeds the latter, the labor supply increases, and *vice versa*. An important component of this hypothesis is that the variation of real wages from what was expected could be perceived. When inflation is low, inflation expectations are low; therefore, an increase in the price level is interpreted as an increase in demand for firms' output. As a result of this perceived increase in real prices, firms respond by increasing output, which can only be done by offering higher wages than anticipated by the workers, thereby inducing the labor to increase its supply. Under unanticipated inflation the response of the firms and workers can be substantial in the short run. In countries with high inflation the response of real wages and output to an increase in the price level would be negligible, if any.

The distinction between anticipated and unanticipated inflation can be taken a step further to consider anticipated or unanticipated changes in the supply of money. When an increase in the supply of money is steady or constant, as Friedman suggests, the expectations about a sudden jump in the supply of money and the pursing inflation is low.[16] Rational expectations hypothesis claims similar insensitivity to other temporary and unexpected occurrences in other economic variables. The policy-related conclusion is that aggregate demand shocks destabilize the economy and that central banks should be independent.

According to Ball, Mankiw, and Romer the fact that there are price rigidities due to implicit contracts, customer markets, and so on does not support the Keynesian theory, because the foundation of that theory is based on the effects of nominal rigidities, while these sources of price rigidities affect real prices and wages.[17]

Real Business Cycle School

Kydland and Prescott offer an explanation of business cycles that is completely based on the supply side of the economy rather than the demand side.[18] Friedman, a monetarist, and Lucas, from the new classical School, both point out that discretionary policies are destabilizing and recommend the use of policies that affect the supply side incentives to create jobs and to dampen business cycles.[19,20] Nevertheless, their explanations and recommendations are only partially based on the supply side. The new theory expands the claims of the previous group of continuous equilibrium theorists by declaring that every phase of any business cycle is indeed at equilibrium. This is in contrast to the neoclassical perspective that recessions are periods of disequilibrium. Although recessions are undesirable they represent profit maximizing behavior at a state of equilibrium. Since the new theory claims that real rather than monetary shocks are the causes of aggregate instability, it is known as the real equilibrium business cycle theory (REBCT), where the word "equilibrium" is commonly omitted in reference. REBCT attributes business cycles to random advances in technology instead of monetary shocks or sticky wages and prices. Tobin, a Keynesian, points out that the "real equilibrium of a full information model could move around, driven by fluctuations in natural endowments, technologies and tastes."[21] For proponents of REBCT, however, sufficient accumulation of such outcomes could resemble a business cycle. This view of business cycles indicates that troughs and peaks represent deviations from trend, so trying to eliminate them is ineffective since they are caused by random events. Instead of trying to eliminate the cycles, it would be better to focus on understanding economic growth in order to improve the lives of the people and learn to live with fluctuations from the trend line.

REBCT is based on the microeconomic foundations of choice theory. It is based on the findings of rational expectations hypothesis, equilibrium modeling analysis, and game theory. The latter explains economic behavior, and hence the outcomes, of the interaction of economic agents, by anticipating the behavior of other agents as well as the behavior of the fiscal and monetary authorities. Two core assumptions of REBCT theory are that changes in technology causes changes in output and that the rate of growth of technology is random with a large variance. Therefore, the "shock" to the economy is initiated from technology and this affects aggregate supply, rather than aggregate demand. Supply side shocks change the structure of the economy and force economic agents to modify their behavior; a rationale that is based on the rational expectations hypothesis and the rules of game theory, which require agents to maximize their utility. Schumpeter states that the effect of long-run changes in technology is growth, but that in the short run it causes disequilibrium, which leads to business cycles.[22]

According to Wicksell trade cycles are functions of supply side shocks to the interest rate and not monetary shocks.[23] Shocks that increase the market interest rate above its natural rate cause endogenous changes in the supply of money throughout the banking system. The cycle is completed by changes in levels of investment and the interest rate until the latter is the same as the natural rate. Wicksell's theory influenced the Austrian school.[24] Keynesian models are also based on real economic variables; however, their orientation is focused on aggregate demand and not the supply side. The source of instability in these theories is the volatility of investment. Although the foundations of the two theories are close, one is based on investment while the other is based on interest rate; the philosophical divide is huge. The works of Wicksell and REBCT of the last quarter of the 20th century focus on the supply side while the works of Samuelson and Keynesians of different flavors are based on demand side.[25,26] The main focus of the Keynesians, however, were improvements in macroeconomic performance via discretionary policy to the point that it was believed that business cycles were no longer a major issue and that they would be eliminated before long. This view was not only shared by Keynesians like Bronfenbrenner, but by the advocates of other schools as well, as shown in the discussion of the automatic stabilizers of Chapter 6.[27]

Blinder points to the oil shocks of 1973 and 1978 as evidence of the role of supply shocks in producing economic instability.[28] The former was the result of a deliberate oil embargo by OPEC, while the latter was the by-product of the uncertainty in the oil market caused by the Islamic revolution of Iran. When the joint attack of Egypt and Syria on Israel in 1973 was defeated, the Arab nations managed to convince OPEC to impose an oil embargo to retaliate against Western support for Israel. The Islamic Revolution of Iran posed the possibility of the closure of the Strait of Hormuz in the Persian Gulf, which would have caused a reduction of almost 20% in the short run supply of oil. The stagflation of the 1970s in the United States demonstrates the inability of Keynesian's aggregate demand analysis.

It is important not to confuse the supply-side-based economic analyses that were utilized by Keynesians,[29] monetarists,[30] and new classicists,[31] with the group that Feldstein[32] calls "new supply-side economists," such as Laffer and Wanniski, who have made unsubstantiated claims of magical powers of tax cuts and deregulations that have become a Republican Party platform.[33]

A major point of REBCT is that business cycles are caused by technology shocks. Since technological innovations are distributed randomly and resemble the statistical concept of random error, they are not explainable; therefore, they cannot be predicted. This is not to refute that business cycles follow long and gradually changing patterns. The gradual movement along a business cycle is due to its long run trend. Once the trend and other explainable components of a business cycle are accounted for, the remaining short-run fluctuations are random. This is also not meant to suggest that their source or origin is unknown. Quite to the contrary, REBCT claims that technological advances are the cause of the random origin of business cycles.

SECTION III

Schools of Thought in Fiscal Theory

CHAPTER 8

New Keynesian School

The stagflation of the late 1960s and inflation of the 1970s discredited Keynesian theories. Theoretical challenges from advocates of monetarism, Austrian economics, and rational expectations hypothesis discredited the notion of a trade-off between unemployment and inflation suggested by the Phillips curve, and cast doubt on the effectiveness and usefulness of discretionary policy, be it fiscal or monetary.[1] In spite of their criticisms of Keynesian economics, monetarists have been influenced by it. One of these influences is evident through the inclusion of interest rate in their explanations of the demand for money. Keynesian economics has been influenced by monetary theory as well. One consequence of the emergence of the above mentioned theories was modifications to Keynesian theory, even the revival of the Phillips curve. An example of the latter is an expectations-augmented Phillips curve model by Gordon.[2]

Important economic theories, like theories in other areas of science, have not been able to explain all phenomena. New economic theories point out the shortcomings of existing ones and provide a plausible answer to remaining questions. Major theories, such as Keynesian or quantity theory, solve many problems and have a greater and longer-lasting impact on the field than minor ones. The revival of Keynesian theory begins with identification of shortcomings of the theories that had become dominant in the 1970s. For example, Tobin points out that real business cycle theory fails to clarify how macroeconomic coordination works.[3] The original Keynesian question regarding the failure of the market economy under certain conditions, and the inability of the invisible hand to coordinate activities of economic agents in such cases, remained unanswered. Prolonged unemployment in Europe discredited the new classical views, while bringing a new life to the possibility of unemployment equilibrium.[4] During the dominance of monetary and other theories, the Keynesians pointed out their agreement with the notion that "money matters," but softly add, "except in deep recessions." While the need for microeconomic theories and the use of a general equilibrium approach are embraced by the new Keynesians, their assumptions concerning perfect information and perfect competition are questionable. The Keynesians, new and old, cannot overlook market imperfections and information asymmetry. The theoretical superiority of rational expectations hypothesis is undeniable, but it does not rule out the existence of sticky prices and wages, which are central to any Keynesian analysis.

The demise of Keynesian economics was similar to that of monetary theory and most other theories with partial applicability. Each theory questions the assumptions of its predecessors and introduces new assumptions to overcome the shortcomings of the former, but still fails to be applicable in all situations, especially in cases that have not emerged yet. Each theory also contains components that fail to match reality; nevertheless, they provide input for newer, more complex, and more advanced theories. An example where a theory fails the reality test and is not supported by evidence is the notion of continuous equilibrium and the associated claim that all unemployment is voluntary.

According to the real business cycle theory, money is neutral and markets adjust internally. The new Keynesian theory asserts that money cannot be neutral due to market imperfections. In this regard, some of the original Keynesian ideas are preserved while a greater role for monetary policy is also accepted. The dispute on the use of a fiscal policy for Keynesians was never whether it should be used solely or whether there was a role for monetary policy, rather it was about the use of discretionary policy versus policy rules.[5] It seems that everyone agrees both demand and supply shocks are destabilizing. The new Keynesians are one of the few groups who argue that the economy cannot reestablish equilibrium itself, that is through some sort of invisible hand mechanism, thus requiring government intervention that necessitates the use of discretionary policy instead of a rule. Government intervention is also deemed necessary due to market imperfections that could be far away from being perfectly competitive or monopolized markets. A more common economic view of existing market reality is the existence of monopolistic competition, which is synonymous with brand names so common in modern economies. For example, the traditional manufacturing brand names that were associated with automobiles and appliances were expanded to encompass consumer goods such as shoes and shirts during the last quarter of the 20th century. The new Keynesian economists also point to the existence of externalities, both positive and negative, which distort market economies and makes resource allocation non-Pareto optimal.

The new Keynesians have examined both nominal and real rigidities in prices and wages. The claim of nominal rigidities of prices and wages dates back to Keynes himself. The claim of such rigidities was based on observations that stem from the lack of a substantial and economy-wide decline in prices and wages during the Great Depression. Wage rigidities are explained, in part, by the existence of contractual agreements that are for periods of a year or longer. In most cases, with the exception of day-workers, temporary employees, and labor contracts with a clause allowing termination without cause, employment contracts are longer than a year. In Europe the presence of stronger and more widespread membership in labor unions provides greater bargaining power and the ability to resist wage reductions. Both labor and employers use their expectations about the future of the economy when they engage in negotiations on wages. Rational expectation hypothesis indicates that on the average these expectations will be correct.

The contribution of the new Keynesians lies in their incorporation of microeconomic foundations into their explanation of these rigidities, rather than applying an arbitrary assumption. The new Keynesians maintain aggregate demand disturbances are the dominant destabilizing force in the economy and claim that the stickiness of wages in the labor market, and prices in the commodity market, indicate that money is not neutral. Downward stickiness of nominal wages means that laborers are unable to realize that as a result of a decline in prices real wages have increased. Of course, when the argument includes downward rigidity of prices then real wages remain unchanged, which justifies laborers' behavior. This situation is what Keynes called unemployment equilibrium. Reluctance to accept lower wages in light of a lack of evidence of price declines is rational behavior. The question is which one should fall first: prices or wages? If one cannot decline unless the other one does then there is a stalemate, and hence an unemployment equilibrium. Early Keynesian models posit that downward rigidity of wages prevents a reduction in costs, thereby making it impossible for prices to adjust downward toward the market-clearing equilibrium in the goods market. Hicks separates the market for labor and most commodities from the financial market.[6] Prices in the latter market are free to adjust, both upward and downward, while prices in the former market are rigid, at least downward.

When the economy is growing the issue is null. In a growing economy an increase in demand necessitates price and wage increases and the market economy then can allocate resources efficiently. However, when economic growth is lacking and the economy is enjoying a state of overall equilibrium without growth the market mechanism fails because there is no way to signal the wishes of consumers and producers. A moderate inflation is preferred to an economy at the state of equilibrium because it allows consumer preferences to be conveyed to entrepreneurs via price signals.

When expansionary monetary policy is anticipated the new Keynesian accepts the rational expectation hypothesis implication that prices and wages are adjusted to their market-clearing levels. This adjustment renders systematic monetary policy ineffective. This is the same outcome as that predicted by rational expectations hypothesis with continuously clearing markets. Once again, the assumptions of the model prove to be its most crucial component with regard to its conclusions and predictions. Consequently, the theory is susceptible to criticism and refutation.

Cost of Living Adjustment Clauses

The assumption of downward rigidity of wages is open to criticism since it lacks theoretical explanations, which has serious implications. The unemployment equilibrium of earlier Keynesians under the assumption of downward wage rigidity implies that people who remain employed receive a real income increase due to a reduction in real prices. In 2008, the worst recession since the Great Depression, unemployment reached 10.1%, which means 89.9% of the labor force was employed and enjoyed an increase in real wages as a result of lower prices. This overwhelming majority, as compared to the unemployed, received gains and should not only be happy but actually promote recessions. This argument ignores the disutility of witnessing the suffering of fellow citizens. Since the magnitude of the utility of lower real wages and the disutility of the misery of a fellow human being are not known *a priori*, the answer to question is not theoretical but empirical.

Another issue worth mentioning is the possibility of having a cost of living adjustment clause (COLA) in labor contracts to avoid the issue of wage rigidity. The advantage of automatic inflation adjustment is that when the prices increase costly labor negotiations can be avoided, which benefits both the employers and the workers. Furthermore, the possibility of a strike or failure of negotiations is avoided. Almost all negotiated labor contracts include periodic increases based on anticipated inflation. At the end of contract periods wages typically have fallen behind inflation and real wages are thus eroded, while at the beginning of the contract period wages are higher than inflation, that is, workers enjoy gains in real wages. Real wages increase right after a new contract due to pressure from labor to recuperate the losses at the end of the previous contract period. Inflation-adjusted contracts can eliminate fluctuations in real wages by automatically modifying nominal wages to maintain constant real wages. Allowances for increases in productivity due to learning or technological advancement can complete the reward mechanism. Another advantage of inflation-adjusted wages is that during recessions downward rigidity of wages can be eliminated. One reason for not having an inflation-adjusted labor contract is that the system will not work when there are supply shocks that increase production costs without having a demand pull. The COLA will trigger wage increases on top of the already increased costs. The result of an increase in prices due to supply shock is a reduction in output. A wage increase will worsen the output shortage caused by the external shock instead of improving it.

Microeconomic Foundations

The discussion of stickiness of wages and prices still lacks theoretical foundations. Except for an argument of the plausibility of wage and price rigidity there is no reason why wages should be rigid or why the rigidity would be toward wage reductions but not wage increases. The theory of imperfect competition or monopolistic competition developed independently by Robinson and Chamberlin provides microeconomic foundations for the new Keynesian's arguments.[7,8] The theory is an integral part of market structure theory in microeconomics but was not used in macroeconomics until the criticism of the new classical and monetary theorists by Keynes.

In an imperfect competition market structure, goods are differentiable; therefore, there is brand recognition. The market for the product consists of few large-size firms with monopoly power over their brand name competing with numerous producers of the good that lack brand name recognition. The production processes for many consumer goods have fit this description since the last quarter of the 20th century. Unlike firms in perfect competition, the firms operating in imperfectly competitive markets make profits, but not as much as the monopolists. The demand is fairly elastic, but not perfectly so. The monopolistically competitive firms can set their prices slightly higher than the market clearing prices, and thus, do not have to reduce their prices as much, if at all, during a recession. Firms operating under imperfect competition face downward sloping demands, similar to that of a monopoly, except flatter. Therefore, a monopolistically competitive firm can increase its prices, although by small margins, but it will lose some revenue as a result. Mankiw and Akerlof and Yellen, and others, claim that under these conditions an increase in cost will result in substantial rigidity in nominal prices.[9,10] Since the main producers under the monopolistic competition are fairly large it will be too expensive for them to change prices in small increments. The costs involved in changing prices include changing orders for purchases and sales, the time and cost of corresponding negotiations, as well as seemingly trivial issues such as creating new price stickers, all of which make prices rigid, both downward as well as upward. Mankiw names these expenditures as "menu costs."[11]

A decline in aggregate demand in the form of a shift will also shift the demand curve for monopolistically competitive firms to the left. Note that the demand curve facing smaller firms is still perfectly elastic. Since the profit margin for monopolistically competitive firms is small, their profit may decline substantially as a result of small changes in demand. This small margin is the reason for the firms' inability to increase their prices by large amounts, or attempt to earn monopoly profits. The profit maximization rule indicates that the price of the firms operating in a market with imperfect competition must fall. However, changing prices will incur "menu costs," thereby reducing profits further. A firm under these conditions might be better off to leave the prices intact, which will result in some loss in profit due to lower demand. The sale of fewer goods provides smaller profits than would have been possible if the menu costs did not exist and the firm could equate its marginal cost with its marginal revenue. Monopolistic competition theory with solid basis in microeconomic theory reflects the reality of the market structure of the last quarter of the 20th century and provides a plausible explanation for price rigidity. The theory provides an explanation for the reduction in output to below the level of full employment output.

When the menu cost is greater than zero, a firm's profit maximizing output is less than the quantity deemed appropriate by society and microeconomic theory, which requires parity between marginal revenue and marginal cost. The result of deviation of output from the optimal level is a deadweight loss to society, the size of which depends on the magnitude of the menu cost. Gordon shows that the deadweight loss also depends on the slope of the marginal cost curve; the steeper the marginal cost curve is, the lesser is the impact of a given menu cost.[12] This means the firm will have less incentive to maintain higher prices; therefore, the deadweight loss to society is lower. Note that the suboptimal behavior of the firm reduces profits but not as much as if the firm reduced its prices, and hence increased its output from a suboptimal position to that of the theoretically appropriate optimal level. However, the loss to society is potentially much larger than the loss to firms because of negative externalities, as demonstrated by Blanchard and Kiyotaki.[13]

Efficiency Wages

Marshall coined the term "efficiency-wages" to name the practice by employers that pay higher wages for better workers.[14] In such cases the result is that a dollar of wage provides the same amount of output regardless of the efficiency of worker. The practice is widespread but is not reflected in marginal analysis, where MC = MR, and the focus is only on the cost and revenue of the last unit produced. Akerlof and Yellen prove that in the presence of efficiency wages in the labor market and imperfect competition in the product market, aggregate demand disturbances might cause business cycles.[15]

Under this theory, rigidity in nominal prices will cause large output fluctuations when nominal aggregate demand shocks occur. This effect will be exacerbated when money wages are also downward-rigid due to contractual agreements, as downward wage rigidities do not allow the MC to adjust when production conditions change. The inefficiencies that arise from these conditions cannot be resolved by internal forces of the economy because the structural foundation of the economy is the source of price and wage rigidities, as explained by imperfect competition. Consequently, it is necessary for the government to intervene in order to dislodge the economy from its unemployment equilibrium and to restore efficiency in the market. This is yet another example of the existence of negative externalities in the market economy. The presence of negative externalities requires government intervention. Accepting government intervention when externalities exist is more common in the case of education but less so when the products are consumer goods.

Other reasons for price rigidities are provided in macroeconomic texts, where they belong. They include sensitivity of marginal costs to procyclical elasticity of demand and fluctuations in output: thick market externalities, customer markets, price rigidity and input–output tables, capital market imperfections, and judging quality by price, to name but a few. The important point for the purpose at hand is to show the possibility of price and wage rigidity based on microeconomic theories and fundamentals. These theories are utilized within the new Keynesian school to provide justification for discretionary policy and evidence of the effectiveness of fiscal policy.

CHAPTER 9

Post Keynesian

Effective Demand

Post Keynesians claim that the foundation of macroeconomic theory is the principle of effective demand, presented by Keynes.[1] The idea is fairly old compared to other fiscal and monetary schools, but the term itself was used by Eichner and Kregel.[2]

According to Keynes the amount of employment is a function of expected earnings under a given state of technology, resource and factor costs, and the level of employment.[3] At the firm level the entrepreneur seeks to "maximize the excess of the proceeds over the factor cost." To determine the output level that maximizes profit Keynes proceeds by defining both aggregate supply and aggregate demand as functions of employment. He focuses on the "proceeds" of output rather than quantity when he refers to aggregate demand. The intersection of demand and supply determines the level of employment that maximizes the income of the entrepreneur, which is often called profit. The intersection point provides the level of employment, which is also the point at which the expected profits of the entrepreneur are maximized. Effective demand for Keynes is the value of the aggregate demand function at the point of intersection with the supply function.

Definition

Effective demand is the value of aggregate demand at the point it intersects with aggregate supply.

Classical economists accept Say's law that "supply creates its demand," which was discussed in detail in Chapter 1. According to Keynes, Say's law implies that the aggregate demand and aggregate supply functions must be equal for all levels of employment. This implies that regardless of the level of employment the aggregate demand price is always equal to the aggregate supply price. The implication is that instead of a single equilibrium price there exist infinite equilibrium prices. Consequently, the amount of employment is indeterminate. The principle of effective demand in this context is the starting point for the advocates of Post Keynesian economists. When an increase in the value of effective demand is no longer accompanied by an increase in output it is possible that full employment has been achieved. At full employment "aggregate employment" is inelastic in response to an increase in the effective demand for its output. This conclusion is the foundation of Say's law, which implies full employment. If the above relationship is not correct then Say's law is disproven.

Keynes refutes the neutrality of money. In classical economics an increase in demand for liquidity, that is money, implies that the money supply increases, as if it is a commodity that can be and is produced in the market economy. Keynes, instead, argues that the elasticity of productivity with respect to money is very small, if not zero. In other words, changes in the supply of money would change output very little, if at all. The classical view implies the neutrality of money, which means that the existence of money does not affect the demand for goods and services. According to Keynes, it is not necessary to earn income or to have saved for current consumption when the banking system is allowed to create money through partial reserve requirements.[4] All that is needed is the expectation of future income. Under this interpretation, an expectation of future earnings is greater than the amount necessary to invest in the production of goods that would generate such earnings. The implication is that an increase in nominal money is capable of increasing (future) real output and employment. Thus, contrary to the claim of classical economists, money is not neutral. This is not the same as the money illusion (see Chapter 7), which states that a response in real variables as a result of a change in nominal variables is due to being fooled. According to Arrow and Hahn, contracts based on nominal money refute the rational expectations equilibrium as well as the existence of a set of prices that would cause equilibrium in all markets.[5] Almost all contracts are based on nominal money, while economic decisions are supposed to be based on real variables. The consequence is the need to form expectations about the future and the outcomes of real variables in the economy. In barter economies, on the other hand, economic decisions depend on real variables since in order to exchange goods in the market it is necessary to have produced something and output is a real variable. In such economies, involuntary unemployment would be meaningless and Say's law could prevail as discussed in Chapter 1. In the modern society, which Keynes calls an entrepreneur economy, contracts are based on nominal money to be earned and paid in the future.

The classical economists believed that the market-based processes can establish a unique equilibrium in the economy. Keynes refutes this gross substitute assumption, which is easier to explain than define. A related "*differentia*" of money for Keynes is that the elasticity of substitution between goods and liquid assets is also nearly zero. The same is true about services as well. The implication is that the portion of income not used for consumption of goods and services ends up as demand for money. In other words, when money appreciates in value there is no substitute for it. This includes investment for the purpose of future consumption. Therefore, one's entire income does not have to be spent on consumption of goods and services, which invalidates Say's law. In classical economics saving implies a time preference for future consumption, but according to the above **gross substitution** effect, this need not be the case.

Definition

Gross substitution is the spillover from adjustments in one market, for example the money market, into another market, for example goods market, by substituting expenditure from one form, that is goods and services, to another form, that is money and assets.

A main concern for the Post Keynesians, as in the case of all advocates of discretionary policy, is market failure in the presence of externalities. Of special interest is the spillover from one market, for example labor, into another market, for example goods. Disequilibrium in one market affects the equilibrium in another market. If the gross substitution assumption is valid then it is possible to have involuntary unemployment, contrary to the claim of the classical economists. The assumption of involuntary unemployment also implies that the gross substitution need not occur between intertemporal consumption, but rather between goods and assets, including liquid money.

Risk in Post Keynesian Models

Entrepreneurs face both uncertainty and risk. In a market economy an entrepreneur is rewarded for planning and executing production, based on their expectation of nominal future incomes and expenditures. Although many writers utilize the terms risk and uncertainty as synonyms, the two are not exactly the same (see Chapter 7). Uncertainty sometimes refers to outcomes that are unknown and occur at random, while risk refers to outcomes that are unknown but occur according to some probability distribution function that has known properties. Therefore, risk can be estimated by an appropriate distribution function that will provide a given probability of occurrence. This use of the term "uncertainty" is similar to that of Keynes where he states: "[uncertainty does] not mean merely to distinguish what is known for certain from what is only probable. The game of roulettes is not subject, in this sense to uncertainty...The sense in which I am using the term is that... there is no scientific basis on which to form any calculable probability whatever. We simply do not know."[6] He proposes that uncertainty does not depend on probability distributions and that economic agents believe that "no expenditure of current resources can provide reliable statistical or intuitive clues regarding future prospects." The implication is that future outcomes are nonergodic, thus making any probabilistic forecast of the future impossible, which denies the possibility of forming rational expectations of the future.

Definition

An **ergodic** process is a process that can be predicted by sampling. This implies that the time path depends on the initial values.

The implication is that economic agents are left with two choices, either make no decisions or follow their "animal spirits."[7] The perspective on uncertainty provides "a more general theory explaining long-run decisions regarding liquidity demands and investment decisions, the existence of long-period underemployment equilibrium, the long-run no-neutrality of money, and the unique and important role Keynes assigned to nominal contracts and especially the money-wage contract."[8] It is noteworthy that Davidson seems to use the term "uncertainty" as equivalent to the term "risk" as defined above.[9]

Decisions in Post Keynesian Models

The assumption of nonergodic outcomes leaves economic agents with an option of taking no action or randomly choosing a decision. The latter is not possible to model and the former is contradictory to the reality where economic agents have to make economic decisions to survive. The Post Keynesian economists argue that all economic activities and their payoffs are separated by time, and that all economic decisions occur under one of three mutually exclusive possibilities:

1. **The Objective Probability:** Rational expectation hypothesis models claim that all outcomes can be learned, and thus predicted, provided the event occurs often enough to allow formation of mathematically based expectations.
2. **The Subjective Probability:** Subjective decisions are personal in nature and may or may not converge to the theoretically correct outcomes. At the current level of statistical technology it is not possible to forecast the outcome of collective subjective decisions, let alone the outcome of an individual decision. However, at least at the macroeconomics level, the importance of being able to forecast individual decisions is of dubious value.
3. **The True Uncertainty:** Post Keynesian economists argue that even if objective probabilities of the rational expectation hypothesis type, or the subjective probabilities of individual instincts, exist, it is still possible that between the decision to take an economic action and the time the process is completed and the payoff is made, changes occur that were unforeseen and unexpected. In fact, they go beyond this analysis and assume there is no way to predict the future. Post Keynesians point to the statement by Keynes that "the hypothesis of a calculable future leads to a wrong interpretation of the principles of behavior" and ignore the advancements in forecasting techniques

since the 1930s. However, to their credit, advancements in forecasting are beneficial for econometric modeling utilized by economists but not for the general public. On the other hand, rational expectations hypothesis does not claim that economic agents actually use sophisticated modeling to forecast the future. Rational expectations hypothesis uses the modeling techniques that model and forecast the behavior of the public. The public forms expectations based on individual experiences that may be subjective. The collective outcome of their behavior, however, is believed to be possible to forecast.

The claim that individuals are unable to form rational expectations that, on the average, are the same as the theoretically predicted outcome, places the cart before the horse. Economic theory is not a phantom of imagination or a creation of economists in ivory towers. Economic theory explains the outcome of the economic conduct of humans, within the norms and institutions that prevail. For example, the rules that apply to an industrial society need not apply in an agrarian society, nor in a barter economy. There is no reason that economic theories that are developed to explain a modern economy would necessarily apply to an agrarian economy. The statistical models are tools to aid economists in forecasting the outcome of economic agents that will occur, regardless of whether we have the tools to forecast them or not.

The Post Keynesians apply the theory of expected utility, which assigns probabilities to a list of mutually exclusive consequences. Under this theory, when an individual cannot specify a complete set of prospects, true uncertainty is created. The ability to assign ranks to the elements of the set is required. The inability to assign ranks can stem from failure to comprehend all the possibilities or incapability of assigning probabilities. Post Keynesians reject the predictability of outcomes in the real goods market, but believe that for subjects such as the existence of money, fixed money contracts, and the legal system that enforces the nominal contracts, it is possible to form expectations about future outcomes. To them, money is the commodity that is used to reconcile all contracts, which are enforced by the civil laws of the land.

The Post Keynesian Legacy

Post Keynesians consider themselves to be the true followers of Keynes and believe that other groups, both supporting and opposing his views, misunderstand him, but not in the same way as Leijonhufvud claimed.[10] Post Keynesians has identified certain concepts in Keynes's work and has made them the center of its school of thought. The notions of uncertainty, the inability to have correct expectations about the future, gross substitution, and money contracts are some examples. One of the major influential contributors to this school is Kalecki, who also contributed to the neo-Marxian groups. The group has also exploited the ideas of Joan Robinson, who was a contemporary of Keynes. Robinson is the foundation of many of the groups that followed Keynes, including New Keynesians, as well as Post Keynesians.[11] The main contribution of Robinson's work is that it provides a microeconomic foundation for the Keynesian price and wage rigidity. The final contemporary of Keynes that has contributed to the school is Kaldor, who supported the notion of predictability in economics, at least in the growth theory.

Both Robinson and Kalecki were socialists; Kaldor has done extensive work in welfare economics. The school had to wait until the 1970s to have additional prominent members, such as Paul Davidson. Although early members of the school like Robinson and Kalecki are considered to have tried to distance themselves from Keynes, the later contributors are trying to claim Keynes' legacy as his "true" followers. Every major theoretical contribution changes economics by incorporating its major contributions into other theories and perspectives, and Keynes's work is no exception. However, since World War II Post Keynesians are trying to return to the original and unmodified concepts in Keynes's work, which often means that other gains in understanding economics are ignored, such as the contributions of the rational expectations hypothesis. Many of the assumptions, analyses, and interpretations of the members of the school since the 1970s have not gained widespread acceptance in academia. There are still traces of welfare orientation in the school, such as support for employment benefits and even actual employment by the government, strict financial regulations, and countercyclical discretionary fiscal policy to reduce the inherent cyclical nature of the market economy production.

SECTION IV
The Evidence

CHAPTER 10

Empirical Evidence Regarding Fiscal Policy

The previous nine chapters provide a minute fraction of what needs to be said about fiscal theory and its policy implications. The focus of the present book has been broad and conceptual. For example, the detailed analytical tools required to apply the theories have been bypassed in favor of rudimentary explanations of the theories and their implications.

Economic theories are formed to explain the economic behavior of humans. There is no economic theory without this human element. It is important to validate economic theories through empirical analysis to provide evidence of the correctness of the theory. Theories are based on assumptions that are believed to be reasonable, meaningful, or axiomatically obvious. For example, it is believed that more is preferred to less on the grounds that if something is desirable at a given level, then more of it should be also desirable. This statement is simplistic in that it will only apply to a limited range of economic behavior. For example, more shoes are preferred to fewer shoes but conceivably there could be a point where one has too many shoes and has exhausted all available space for storing them in a dwelling. Another example is overconsumption of food. In chemistry, it is said that every substance becomes toxic at some dose. Many young people discover this reality after having too much to drink.

Sometimes evidence may not support a theory because the theory is incorrect, while at other times the lack of evidence is due to faulty assumptions. No one necessarily behaves according to the assumptions or logic of a theory. However, theories are acceptable as long as they provide sufficient evidence that they can explain observable reality. Sometimes theories fail to explain new realities because of changes in the economy or in economic agents' behavior. In this chapter we will provide some of the more compelling evidence in support of fiscal policy as well as its shortcomings. We will avoid giving a laundry list of articles that test the validity of theories and their assumptions, since that would take several volumes and is of dubious benefit for the present focus. Instead, attention is focused on only a few major works and the overall state of our understanding of the role of fiscal policy and its instruments in the economy.

The effectiveness of discretionary policy is as important as the correctness of the theory. In order for discretionary policy to be effective it must elicit the correct and anticipated outcome in a timely fashion. The policy must yield its desired outcome in less time than the length of a half a phase of a cycle; otherwise the economy will move to the next phase of the cycle and the policy not only becomes ineffective, but also inappropriate. A phase of the cycle is the distance between one peak or trough to the next peak or trough. In other words, the shorter the outside lag of a policy the more preferred is the policy. Unless the policy is automatically activated it is necessary that the sum of the inside and outside lag be less than half of a phase of the cycle. It is also necessary to know the magnitude of the response to a given amount of change in the policy instrument. Finally, it is necessary to be able to determine the position of the economy on the business cycle. Without this information and knowledge it would not be possible to use fiscal policy to achieve a desired outcome.

Since there are different instruments at the disposal of a policymaker the answer to the above questions must be determined for all instruments. When dealing with multiple instruments it is necessary to determine which one is more effective or appropriate for a particular situation.

Empirical Evidence for Keynesian Theory

The 1960s witnessed intense debates on fiscal and monetary policies. Theoretical discussions indicated that many of the outcomes depend on specific circumstances, and thus, were a matter of empirical study. The proponents of each theory provided numerous empirical evidences for their ideologies. One area of debate focused on the relationship between consumption and income because consumption is a component of aggregate demand, an idea championed by Keynes as a factor that could explain business cycles. On the monetary side, Friedman offered the permanent income hypothesis.[1] Alternatively, Ando and Modigliani and

Brumberg counter Friedman by proposing the life cycle hypothesis in support of the Keynesian theory.[2,3] The implication of the latter hypothesis is that the rate of growth of national income determines national savings, which is demonstrated in the works of Modigliani, as well as others. Under this hypothesis, the faster an economy grows the higher the rate of saving will be. The life cycle hypothesis has microeconomic foundations, which are extended to macroeconomics by Modigliani and Brumberg.[4] Ando and Modigliani expand the macroeconomic version, which became the foundation of the Federal Reserve-MIT-Penn large-scale macro-econometric model.[5] The customary consumption models of the 1970s are the result of combining the life cycle and permanent income hypotheses with modifications based on other empirical works. These studies support the notion that national savings is a function of the growth rate of the economy as well as population growth. A revised version of the life cycle hypothesis, in which consumers maximize their utility by considering their own consumption as well as the utility of their offspring, is suggested by the Ricardian equivalence hypothesis of Barro.[6] However, productivity decline in the 1970s casts doubt on the validity, or at least generalizability, of the hypothesis. Furthermore, the decline in savings rates in the United States cannot be explained by changes in its economy and population, and therefore, other factors are needed to provide an acceptable explanation.

Discretionary Policy and Aggregate Demand

The entire subject of fiscal policy would be meaningless if fiscal policy could not affect the economy. Advocates of fiscal policy claim that it affects the economy by influencing aggregate demand. Recall that fiscal policy was originally designed to remedy recessions. Buiter and Tobin investigate whether fiscal policy has any impact on aggregate demand; in specific they investigate whether there is a difference in the short run, long run, and cumulative effects.[7] The impetus for the study is the monetarists' claim that fiscal policy is ineffective and does not change aggregate real demand, nominal income, or the price level, and that the quantity of money is the primary source of changes in the economy. Buiter and Tobin's main focus is to determine whether fiscal policy is ineffective, rather than to measure the extent of its importance. They point out that the extent of the effectiveness of any policy, including fiscal policy, depends on how far the economy is from its full employment level. The larger the disequilibrium is the more effective the tool(s) will be. Recall from Chapter 3 that the extent of the effectiveness of monetary and fiscal policy depends on the responsiveness of the LM and IS schedules; that is, on the slopes of the two curves. Monetary policy is most effective when the LM curve is vertical and IS curve is flat, while the opposite is true for the fiscal policy. It seems, at least for the sake of debate, that the two groups claim that their heralded policy tool is more effective regardless of the slopes of the IS and LM curves. According to Buiter and Tobin short-term effects are easier to detect, since in order to measure the long-term effect, either no other factor affecting the economic phenomenon of interest, such as aggregate demand, should change, or an effective way of isolating the effect of a fiscal change must be devised for such purpose. They also state that it is important to distinguish between stock variables, such as the accumulated effect of debt, and flow variables, such as government budget and deficit. They argue changes in stock variables should and do have more persistent effects than changes in flow variables.

Empirical Evidence for Phillips Curve

One of the strongest pieces of evidence in support for discretionary policy is provided by Phillips, who empirically demonstrates the link between unemployment and inflation.[8] The established trade-off implies a policy option suggesting that the government can choose policies to exchange unemployment for inflation and *vice versa*. By manipulating fiscal and monetary policies the government can substitute one unpleasant outcome for another. During transition periods both unemployment and inflation would be low and tolerable. This notion led to the concept of fine-tuning, which implies the possibility of prolonging the periods of low inflation and unemployment, while reducing or even eliminating high values of both. Some economists, most notably Tobin, subscribed to some version of this notion, while others such as Friedman and Lucas discounted these possibilities, based on their respective theoretical and ideological stances.

One problem with the Phillips curve is that people will learn from previous inflations caused by expansions in monetary or fiscal policies. A common modeling practice to establish causality is to include lagged variables.[9] Taylor and Calvo employ a rational expectations model with a leading inflation variable to represent anticipated inflation.[10,11] Such formulations are designed to test New Keynesian's interpretation of the existence of the Phillips curve. Rudd and Whelan discount the ability of lagged inflations' ability to predict future values of real variables.[12]

The empirical correlation between inflation and unemployment, which at first seemed to be a breakthrough for interventionist views, was questioned on theoretical grounds beginning in the 1960s. The fallacy of the relationship is demonstrated by the rational expectations hypothesis. However, the emergence of the New Keynesian school has reignited the debate by providing new explanations and more importantly, new evidence based on more complex statistical procedures. However, the theoretical implications of the existence of an inverse relationship between unemployment and inflation are dire, and so the debate continues.

The new Keynesian Phillips curve is not utilized as a policy instrument as the original Phillips curve was during the 1960s. Rather, it is a way of identifying and signaling the occurrence of inflation.[13] However, their central question concerns what monetary policy should be in response to inflation. Gali and Gertler avoid adopting an *ad hoc* assumption of price stickiness and instead use the concept of marginal cost to describe inflation dynamics successfully.[14]

There are several shortcomings of these models. For example, they cannot explain the perseverance of inflation in the United States; delays in response to monetary shocks; or unorthodox and unexpected outcomes such as the possibility that a credible plan to reduce inflation could result in an expansion instead of a contraction in the economy.[15–17]

Empirical Evidence for Post Keynesian

One of the premises of the proponents of interventionists is that the Fed makes decisions and intervenes in the economy in response to economic conditions. Nevertheless, distinctions among them exist regarding the appropriate choice of variables, what causes increases in money, and whether the Fed directly controls supply of money. For example, the orthodox Post Keynesians use interest rates, the expected inflation rate, the output gap, and levels of aggregate supply and demand, while others claim that the liquidity needs of firms guide the Fed.[18] This group emphasizes the demand for money. Cutler finds little evidence that raw material and capital costs impact the supply of money, especially when using the M2 definition of money.[19] However, the results differ depending on how data are grouped into different segments. When using the M1 definition there is some evidence of influence from the wage bill, which is usually an average of earnings. He finds that the Fed is sensitive to the possibility of inflation, which should not be surprising because of the period under study.

It is one thing to verify that changes in the supply of money cause inflation, it is something else entirely to identify what causes changes in the supply of money itself. This is at the heart of the question of whether the supply of money is endogenous or exogenous. Moore[20] examines the two pillars of the quantity theory of money:

a) Monetary changes are the dominant *cause* of changes in nominal income swamping the temporary and minor influence of fiscal changes.

b) There is no long-run, stable trade-off between inflation and unemployment; that is, the natural rate of unemployment hypothesis is valid.

Changes in the rate of monetary growth cannot cause the rate of unemployment to diverge permanently from its "natural rate," except under conditions of continuously accelerating inflation.

Moore argues that the objective of the Federal Open Market Committee is to stabilize financial markets.[21] Therefore, he studies the extent that the Federal Reserve System accommodates nominal wage increases through policies that change the high-powered monetary base. He utilizes different transformations of the data and finds that wages change the supply of high-powered money, when monthly data are used. The causality conclusion is based on the fact that all independent variables are lagged one period. He also obtains an inverse relationship between the supply of high-powered money and unemployment, but since the statistical significance is low, he concludes that wages are "responsible for monetary accommodation," which is not necessarily true. Quarterly data yield similar results. Moore argues that since labor productivity is also a function of wages it is rigid downward. Since cuts in nominal wages might lead to riots they are not touched even when there is excess supply of labor, that is, unemployment. A conclusion of the study is that since the Fed accommodates the market, monetarists' claim that the supply of money is exogenous is incorrect.

In summary, Post Keynesians claim that there is a difference between borrowed and nonborrowed money and that they are not substitutes. Borrowed money is generated within the banking system by borrowing the funds from people with excess funds and lending it to those in need of funds. The consequence of borrowed money is that its expansionary impact is offset by the contractionary effect of increased debt, a point that Keynes makes. Another important result obtained by the Post Keynesians is the endogeneity of the supply of money.[22] Their recommendation is to explore the nature of the interactions among economic variables and changes in supply of money. The process of establishing the endogeneity of the money supply is supported by evidence based on firm-level cost.

Blinder *et al.* address the issue of price stickiness by asking the CEOs of U.S. firms.[23] Many of the findings are contrary to economic theories. For example, only 11% of firms state that increasing marginal costs and fixed costs are significant in the operation of a firm. These findings do not contradict microeconomic theory when the firm is at the lower end of its production level. An increase in output under these conditions will increase profits. These findings are also compatible with a monopolistic competition market structure where firms are producing below their profit maximizing capacity. A main finding is that prices are sticky because of contracts. Skott and Zipperer find evidence to support the views of Robinson and Kaldor via simulation, but not empirically.[24] Their model, however, does not include public sector, trade, or external shocks.

Empirical Evidence for New Keynesian

One objective of the New Keynesians is to demonstrate the plausibility of price rigidity and that the magnitude of friction need not be great. One consequence of these aims is that nominal demand shocks, regardless of their origin, can affect real variables. Mankiw, Akerlof and Yellen, and Blanchard and Kiyotaki demonstrate that a small price rigidity combined with imperfect competition can cause a proportionately much larger economic effect.[25-27] The latter also argue that since the macroeconomic effects of nominal rigidity of prices is greater than its effect on individual firms, aggregate demand externalities must exist. The externality arises because rigidity in the price-setting behavior of a firm causes rigidity in the price-setting behavior of other firms, which eventually causes rigidity in all prices. An argument for the stickiness of prices is that the cost of changing prices prohibits frequent price adjustment, which is referred to as menu costs. McCallum claims that menu costs are endogenous and there is an inverse relationship between inflation and menu costs, therefore, prices change more frequently in inflationary periods.[28] Consequently, the extent of a relationship between changes in supply of money and changes in real variables depends on the extent of endogeneity of menu costs. The literature uses this inverse relationship to test the New Keynesian theory. The few studies using this approach are methodologically flawed and cannot be used as evidence to support or refute the theory. For example, Defina applies 43 identical regression models to 43 countries but does not utilize a seemingly unrelated regression or panel data methodology.[29] He finds that in 13 cases the relationship is negative and statistically significant. However, the lack of evidence could be due to either poor statistical design or inaccuracy of the theory. There is a vast literature in statistics and econometrics that address the negative consequences of performing multiple regressions instead of more appropriate methodologies that incorporate the entire data set.

Ball, Mankiw, and Romer demonstrate that inflation increases the frequency of price adjustment even under a rigid price environment.[30] The results are robust and provide evidence in support of a Phillips curve–type relationship that is affected by the average rate of inflation. They refute the new classical theory's claim of the existence of a trade-off between aggregate demand and average inflation.[31] They also find evidence to support the Keynesian notion that during contractionary times rents are higher for wages than during expansionary periods. In a comment to the article, Akerlof, Rose, and Yellen question the robustness of the finding, at least for some of the conclusions.[32]

Illusion

The argument against the existence of money illusion is that people rely on real, rather than nominal values when making economic decisions. Advocates of monetary policy do not believe in the existence of a money illusion since it is illogical. Government bonds have two effects: on the one hand bond holders believe they are wealthier, but on the other hand an increase in national debt implies an inevitable increase in taxes in the future; thus real income and wealth will be reduced. The discussion is valid at the macro level. At the micro level, bond holders pay a fraction of the increase in national debt while simultaneously benefitting from the entire increase in wealth. A typical Keynesian argument about bonds is that an increase in bond holdings represents an increase in wealth. The expected future increase in taxes has no impact on current wealth and only implies that in the future, funds will be transferred from tax payers to holders of bonds. On the contrary, Barro refutes the possibility of exchanging bond values with taxes in his Ricardian equivalence hypothesis.[33]

Feldstein and Johnson provide evidence in support of the notion that bonds are perceived as wealth, while Evans and Kroy and McMillin provide evidence in support of the possibility that debt does not represent net wealth.[34-37] Vaughn and Wagner propose a compromise through the notion of debt illusion.[38]

Dalamagas provides empirical support for the theory of debt illusion and addresses the issue of fiscal effectiveness by using a rational expectations model to optimize consumer behavior based on a sample of six developed countries.[39] He finds that consumers ignore the inevitable future tax increases necessitated by current government debt.

Autonomous Expenditures

Friedman and Meiselman provide evidence that the supply of money is better able to explain consumption than autonomous expenditures, which might not be effective at all.[40]

Definition

Autonomous expenditures are expenditures that do not depend on income or production. Each sector of consumption, investment, government expenditures, and net exports is assumed to have a component that is a function of income, or production, and a portion that is not.

The study sparked numerous responses from Keynesians. Ando and Modigliani criticize the methodology of the study and point out that the use of simple correlation when there are numerous factors affecting the endogenous variable is inappropriate and causes misspecification error.[41] The choice of variables and exclusion of outliers such as war years are also questioned. Ando and Modigliani also point out that the use of the most simplistic definition of an endogenous variable while ignoring the underlying assumptions of the theory is not wise.[42] DePrano and Mayor[43] provide the following insightful example:

"Let us compare two theories, one asserting that heavy objects drop faster than light one, and one asserting that they fall equally fast. If we take simple versions of these two theories which make no assumption about the absence of air pressure, and test them by dropping a lead ball and a feather from a tower, the theory that heavy objects fall faster will surely emerge the winner."

Ando and Modigliani show that changing the definition of the variables and utilizing more realistic models changes the outcome, which provides more support for the Keynesian claim than the monetary approach. These alternative models provide better results than Friedman and Meiselman when similar treatments of war years are incorporated. DePrano and Mayor also draw attention to that, theoretically, the supply of money is not exogenous. They test several alternative hypotheses and conclude the following:

1. Consumption can best be explained by the stock of money where money includes time deposits.
2. Consumption can best be explained by autonomous expenditures defined as net investment in producers' durable equipment, nonresidential construction, residential construction, inventory changes, government deficit on income and product account, and net foreign

investment. This is the FM [Friedman and Meiselman] interpretation of the Keynesian hypothesis.

3. Consumption can best be explained by autonomous expenditures defined as investment in producers' durable equipment, nonresidential construction, residential construction, federal government expenditures on income and product account, and exports. One variant of this hypothesis subtracts capital consumption estimates, and the other does not. This is our hypothesis.

The results obtained by Hamburger support some of the arguments set forth by Friedman with regard to the stability of the velocity of money, but he, too, uses the M2 definition, while Moore finds evidence that M2 only accounts for 30% of variation in velocity when monthly data are used. The use of quarterly data reduces the explanatory power to 11%.[44,45]

Crowding Out

A criticism of fiscal policy is that the government activities crowd out the private sector. When a government issues bonds, it is actually borrowing from the public. The return to bonds must be attractive enough in order for the government to be able to divert loanable funds from other uses to the bonds. For a given interest rate, the lower the price of a bond, the higher is its rate of return. Alternatively, for a given price of a bond, the higher the interest rate the greater the return. Unless the total value of a specific bond is small the government must make its rate of return more attractive than the prevailing interest rate. Therefore, the outcome of government decisions to issue bonds causes an increase in the interest rate. The interest rate also increases due to depletion of available funds in the market that are diverted to the purchase of bonds. Of course, the Fed can take counter measures to nullify the consequences, but that is a special case and of little practical value. In general, combining fiscal and monetary policies would increase their effectiveness in achieving policy objectives. According to Arestis and Sawyer, there is another reason for crowding out, which "arose from a combination of the notion of a supply-side equilibrium and that the level of aggregate demand would adjust to be consistent with that supply-side equilibrium."[46] In the context of an exogenous money supply, this adjustment comes through a "real balance" effect, with changes in the price level generating changes in the real value of the stock of money. In turn, changes in real balances generate changes in the level of aggregate demand. In the context of endogenous money, it would come through the adjustment of the interest rate by the Central Bank. This would occur, as indicated above, if the Central Bank adopts some form of "Taylor's rule," provided, of course, interest rates are effective in that regard.[47] As has been argued above, fiscal policy has an effect on the level of aggregate demand, and "crowding out" only occurs if it is assumed that the supply-side equilibrium must be attained (in order to ensure a constant rate of infla-tion), and the level of aggregate demand would in any case be equivalent to the supply-side equilibrium. A final source of crowding out is from the "Ricardian equivalence" as discussed earlier in the chapter.

It seems that the higher the government debt is the greater the crowd-ing out effect should be. Clark refers to the 1820s of England, during which the British government debt was 2.3 times its GNP.[48] He estimates the returns on private assets in England between 1725 and 1839 to deter-mine the extent of the reduction in private investment as a result of the deficit. A common practice is to use the net receipts from debt sales to measure the extent of crowding out. However, Clark uses the market value of the debt. He finds little evidence of foreign financing of the debt and determines that "neither the government deficits nor the mounting debt displace much private investment."

CHAPTER 11

Conclusion

As in other sciences, economic theories depend on the assumptions that are used in their formation. Even the simplest economic concepts are based on specific assumptions. For example, the downward sloping demand curve is based on the assumption that the good is not a Giffen good. One might consider cases such as Giffen goods as exceptions to the rule, which exist in every branch of science. However, attempting to test the validity of a theory without consideration of its assumptions is misleading. Recall from Chapter 10 the importance of assuming the existence of a vacuum and a lack of friction in the physics theory that claims all objects fall at the same rate. Examinations of economic theories without regard to the underlying assumptions are also misleading. In addition, economic events and factors that affect them are stochastic or random and are therefore subject to probabilistic outcomes.

Theories in many disciplines contradict each other and economic theories are no exception. This is not to say that there are no theories that are accepted by the majority, if not all, economists. One example is that the supply curve is upward sloping. Even in cases when consensus exists, the slope or the degree of responsiveness of the phenomenon to its determining factors might be disputed by different theories belonging to different schools of thought. Customarily, it is expected that theories be logical, plausible, coherent, and internally consistent. Otherwise, the theory is easily rejected. The differences in the outcomes of theories stems from differences in their assumptions and which influential factors are incorporated into them. The presence of competing theories with drastically different consequences is common in fields where experimental studies are either not possible or impractical. For example, it is not possible to conduct an experiment in astronomy by creating several universes and subjecting them to different treatments to test the validity of theories pertaining to the birth and development of universe.

Anytime a theory involves human subjects, it is more difficult, or in some cases impossible, to conduct tests based on experimental design because of ethical considerations and the willpower of human subjects. For example, in order to examine the consequence of an increase in the supply of money it is necessary to have a control group within the economy and at least one treatment group, where the latter is subject to a change in the supply of money while the former is not; all other aspects of the lives of the two groups are kept identical. One might be tempted to study a single country over several years and compare the outcome of an increase in the supply of money by comparing the years before and after the change. Unfortunately, this will not work because the supply of money is constantly changing in every economy; therefore, there are no before and after cases to be studied. Sometimes a major change in the supply of money occurs due to a dramatic situation or a significant policy change, but by virtue of being an exception, it is not possible to test any of the existing theories on the supply of money using such a change because the theories are for the general case and not the exception. Note that it is not possible to test a theory about the general conduct and response of an economy using an exceptional situation. To complicate the situation, we know that human beings respond differently to an increase in the supply of money depending on their belief of whether or not the change is temporary, as explained by the permanent income hypothesis. Furthermore, it is necessary to assure that the assumptions of each theory are met before one can conduct the experiment. In fields of study that involve human beings and deal with a multitude of factors, it is impossible in most cases, if not all, to control for all relevant factors as required in experimental design. Recall how the outcome of the experiment on the law of falling objects pivots on the assumption of a lack of atmospheric pressure. In other words, the law is valid only in a vacuum. In studies involving human beings the influencing factors are numerous and customarily impossible to control by the research.

Another factor that complicates testing the validity of theories in economics is that everything in economics is related to everything else. If there is a general rule in economics it is that there is no general rule. This statement is more valid for empirical evidence than theory. Theories, and thus models, depend on *ceteris paribus*, or "other things being equal."

For example, an increase in supply of money is said to reduce its price, which is the interest rate, provided other things remain the same as before the increase in the supply of money. However, it is possible that when the supply of money increases the velocity of money changes instead of the interest rate. The outcome of this increase in the money supply will be different depending on whether the velocity increases, remains constant, or decreases. Note that the velocity of money is assumed to remain constant when the supply of money changes. Yet, a change in velocity is certainly possible, both because of economic reasons as well as the fact that different people might interpret the causes and the consequences of changes in the supply of money differently at different times, and hence respond differently to the same change in the supply of money, thus, causing alternative outcomes.

One way of dealing with assumptions in econometrics is to include the variables that are believed to have an impact on the response variable in the model. These variables are also called control variables but they are not the same as the control variable in an experimental design. In an experimental design study subjects are selected according to a predetermined procedure. Some, at random, are not treated at all while the others are subjected to different treatments of interest. Since the original subjects are chosen at random the averages of grouping different subjects should differ from each other only by a magnitude no larger than what can be attributed to random error. Consequently, any difference between the control group and the treatment group(s) can be attributed to treatment(s) only. The control variables in econometrics, however, are not controlled for anything at all. They are observations that were subject to the same economic forces that affect the response variable. Their inclusion in the model accounts for some of the changes in the response variable; thus, it is claimed that the model has controlled for the effects of these variables. Therefore, the control variables in econometric modeling are considerably different than those in experimental design.

It is important to restate the fact that the control variables in econometric models are also affected by the same forces in the economy that affect the response variable. Furthermore, other exogenous variables in an econometric model are also subject to the same forces and are correlated with the so called control variables, causing multicollinearity. One consequence of multicollinearity is that the actual effect of an exogenous variable is not simply the magnitude of its coefficient. Consequently, its true impact on the response variable cannot be isolated and determined independently from other exogenous variables. Another issue caused by multicollinearity is that some variables that are expected to affect the response variable based on theory may in fact fail to be statistically significant in the presence of another variable or variables with which they are correlated. For example, the variable representing education might be statistically insignificant in explaining income in the presence of a gender or race variable. On the other hand, the exclusion of a gender and race variable would make the education variable statistically significant. However, not controlling for gender or race is not defendable since a test of equality of means income for different races and genders will indicate significant differences exist between them. Furthermore, excluding a variable that actually belongs to the model causes misspecification and estimation bias. It is also possible that different combinations of variables will explain the response variable to different degrees, one of which will be higher and seem to be better. However, changes in the data points used in the analysis will most likely change the explanatory power of the model. In other words, when new data becomes available the inclusion of this new data could yield a different "best model" and possibly a different set of explanatory variables.

The presence of multicollinearity is a serious problem for economic studies because having the correct signs and magnitudes of coefficients is essential in determining the validity of theories. Since under multicollinearity the coefficients are meaningless by themselves, placing too much stock in the magnitudes of the coefficients would be misguided. Furthermore, the inclusion or exclusion of other variables affects the coefficients of variables of interest, which exacerbates the difficulty of determining which theory is supported or refuted by the empirical analysis. The presence of multicollinearity is one explanation for the existence of numerous empirical works in many areas of economics, especially in studies that address fiscal and monetary theory, where different sets of variables are used to explain a given theoretical question.

In the presence of multicollinearity, different sets of collinear variables are capable of providing similar degrees of explanatory power for a model.

Consequently, different studies are able to present reasonable estimations of various outcomes using different sets of variables. A common problem among studies afflicted with multicollinearity is that they provide poor forecasts and that they are not robust. Consequently, empirical studies using different sets of variables and/or periods of data provide contradictory conclusions. One way to check for robustness of the results is to add new data when it becomes available, or to delete data that has become too old. Older data are expected to have less impact as time passes, which justifies their exclusion. The inclusion or exclusion of new data should not change the coefficients by much. Specifically, the significance or lack thereof, and the sign of the coefficient, should remain the same. In economics, changes in the magnitude of coefficients should not change their elasticity, which would imply a substantially different outcome. For example, a small change in a coefficient could change the perception a good from being a normal good to a luxury or inferior good.

Theories are broad while empirical models must be specific. For example, in the quantity theory the quantity of real money multiplied by velocity is equal to the value of transactions in an economy in one year, as depicted by the equation of exchange. This theory does not specify the particular variable that should be used for money. In practice, there are several variables that could be used to represent money, such as M1, M2, and M3; only one of these alternative variables can be used in an empirical study. Consequently, at least three different models can be formulated, one for each of the three response variables, to test the merit of the quantity theory. One would expect that the results should be similar; however, in reality the set of variables that explain M2 need not and in fact do not explain M1 or M3 well. There are many alternative options for each of independent variables as well. Assume that there are k variables that are believed to explain a single response variable. Let each of these variables have n_i alternative choices. For example, in the case of human capital one can use the median years of schooling, percent of people over 25 with high school, baccalaureate, masters, or Ph.D., average number of schooling, and so forth. The number of alternative models that can be utilized will be a staggering number obtained by:

$$N = n_1 \times n_2 \times \ldots \times X \, n_k$$

Assuming $k = 5$, $n_1 = 4$, $n_2 = 3$, $n_3 = 6$, $n_4 = 4$, and $n_5 = 5$, the number of different models that can be established will be:

$$N = 4 \times 3 \times 6 \times 4 \times 5 = 1440$$

The above number is obtained by assuming that all the models use all the variables. In practice any subset of available variables can be used, and usually there are much more than five variables that are considered relevant in many economic studies.

The practice of having different numbers of variables in models that are used to test a particular theory introduces the concern of misspecification. Misspecification occurs when there are too many or too few variables than the correct number of variables. When variables that belong to a model are excluded the type of misspecification is known as the problem of omitted variables. When there are omitted variables the coefficients of the included variables are biased, which means that the expected value of the estimated coefficient is not equal to the true parameter that is estimated. In the presence of multicollinearity the particular set of variables that provides the "best fit" need not include all the theoretically expected factors or control variables, which makes it difficult to determine if the model is misspecified, and if so, what the extent of misspecification is and whether it is the case of an omitted variable or the inclusion of an irrelevant variable.

A review of the literature reveals that numerous studies have a myriad of variables. For example, DePrano and Mayer use 20 different definitions of autonomous variables alone.[1] Of course this article is not an exception; although many articles might use fewer definitions of a particular variable, the use of different combinations of multiple variables is common in most studies. The practice of applying numerous tests using the same data causes another problem. The problem is similar to the issues that arise in multiple comparisons in experimental design studies, when the averages of many variables are compared for equality. In studies where the hypothesis that all variables are equal is rejected it is necessary to conduct pairwise comparisons, to identify which averages are the same and which ones are different. It can be shown that in the cases of repeated tests using the same data the probability of type I error increases to a much higher level than intended. Type I error is the error of rejecting the null hypothesis when the null hypothesis is in fact true. It is necessary to divide the desired probability of type I error by the number of comparisons and use the much smaller probability as the basis of inference. The procedure is commonly known as the Bonferroni correction.

Another problem that afflicts studies of fiscal and monetary theory involves the nature of assumptions, both in theoretical and empirical studies. An important example is the assumption of the exogeneity of the supply of money. In many theories and empirical research the supply of money is depicted as a vertical line, indicating it is exogenous. There are two justifications for this assumption. First, the Fed can set the supply of money at any level that it desires. Second, in the short run the supply of money cannot be changed, at least not by a noticeable amount. The second justification might be plausible if there are rigidities in the market. However, the money market is one of the more responsive sectors of the economy, if not the quickest to respond to changes in the market. The response of the money market can be very rapid, especially if expectations have been heightened due to repeated use of discretionary policies, as set forth by the Rational Expectations hypothesis.

The first justification is even less realistic. The Fed employs numerous economists to gauge economic conditions in order to be able to determine the appropriate amount of supply of money. The members of Board of Governors of the Fed are appointed for 14-year terms to shield them against retaliation by the executive branch of the government. Therefore, there is less chance that the board would arbitrarily set the supply of money under political pressure or due to a lack of knowledge about the economy. The supply of money also depends on the amount of money created by the banking system, which is controlled through the reserve requirement and the overnight interest rate, both of which are determined by the Fed. It is plausible for the conduct of the banking system to be endogenous to the system and to depend on economic forces. For example, after the 2008 recession in the United States the lowering of the interest rate to around zero percent by the Fed could not induce banks to lend more money, nor for the public to borrow more. The power of the Fed to "control" the supply of money is similar to the power of parents in controlling their children; the influence is high and strong but not ultimate. Attempts by the central bank to set the interest rate at its equilibrium level fails because the central bank of a country does not know how to determine the equilibrium interest rate any more than economists in a centrally planned economy would.

There are several obstacles that limit the effectiveness of fiscal and monetary policies. First, it is difficult to determine the exact position of the economy on a business cycle, in part due to the lag in collecting and analyzing the relevant data. Second, after determining the gap between the target and the actual state of the economy, it is difficult to prescribe the correct dose of the instrument. The exact relationship between policy instruments and economic outcomes are not known precisely. Third, legislating and incorporating the prescribed solution takes time, especially if it involves major decisions such as changing taxes or national debt; this is the "inside lag." Fourth, the length of time for realization of the full effect of policy instruments on the economy is not known, and evidence suggests that its variance is substantial; this is the "outside lag." Fifth, the reaction of economic agents to a particular change in policy instrument is not always the same and depends on different economic conditions, as well as how often the policy instrument has been utilized before, the state of the economy, the political climate of the nation, and the expectations of economic agents. These issues convinced Milton Friedman to recommend a constant growth rate for money in lieu of applying discretionary fiscal and/or monetary policies. It is possible that the effectiveness of policy instruments cannot be determined and that their use only exacerbates economic fluctuations. The evidence indicates that outcomes of policy decisions can be forecasted; however, the quality of such forecasts is not satisfactory. This indicates that the current state-of-the-art techniques for diagnosing economic problems and prescribing their solutions are not adequate. The solution to the problem is to utilize fiscal and monetary tools cautiously, and with full transparency. The process of improving analytical capabilities should continue until reasonable forecasts could be made of the outcomes of different policies. There is no known solution for the problem when the inherent variances of different stages of the process are substantial.

As noted above, numerous issues determine the final estimate or forecast in an empirical study of fiscal or monetary policy. Variations in modeling, variables, length of period under study, and choice of what should be declared as unusual cases, and therefore be excluded from the data set, as well as a host of other factors, such as the frequency of wielding a policy, recent history of policy uses, and expectations of economic agents, affect the magnitudes of coefficients in econometric models, as well as their statistical significance. This in turn might signal the effectiveness, or lack thereof, of fiscal or monetary policy. While hardliners of the fiscal and monetary camps might argue that one or the other policy is effective or ineffective, the majority of economists would argue that both policies are important, to some extent. Middle of the road economists might argue the point that one or the other policy is more effective, thus, making the argument an issue of the degree of effectiveness, as in the live debate of Milton Friedman and Walter Heller on November 14, 1968, during the Seventh Annual Arthur K. Salomon Lecture at the New York University, even though both presenters were considered to have orthodox views in their respective beliefs. The statement of Alfred Marshall about the importance of supply or demand might be useful in response to the question of the effectiveness of fiscal and monetary policy. Marshall resembled the effectiveness of supply and demand to the cutting ability of a pair of scissors where the combined actions of both blades are necessary to cut. In the case of fiscal and monetary policy it is possible to exercise one without the other one. The history since the 1930s indicates that pure fiscal or monetary policy without the presence of the other is rare, if it ever existed. In modern economies, both fiscal and the monetary policies are utilized, although not necessarily to the same extent, or simultaneously, to achieve governments' economic, social, and political objectives. The degree of utilization of one policy or the other is reflective of the normative values of policymakers and economists in charge of the appropriate institutions, and often their constituents. The discussions in this book and the empirical evidence indicate that neither policy can be implemented with scientific precision and the assurance of a specific outcome. An effective approach would be to utilize all the available tools to achieve the desired objectives. At a minimum, this will allow the use of a specific instrument to be more effective, even with a lower dosage.

Some economic objectives are similar. For example the objective of increasing output, or gross domestic product (GDP), is the same as reducing unemployment. A reduction in unemployment increases output, but the same outcome could be achieved by increasing output, which would reduce unemployment. To achieve either objective, the more effective method is the use of expansionary fiscal or monetary policy, notwithstanding the argument that discretionary policy is ineffective. In this regard, fiscal and monetary policies are similar. However, the complete impacts of the two policies are not identical in all aspects. In addition to an increase in output and a reduction in unemployment, the outcome of an expansionary fiscal policy is that the interest rate will also increase. However, for an expansionary monetary policy, the increase in output and reduction in unemployment are accompanied by a reduction in the interest rate. An increase in the interest rate benefits lenders, while a decrease in it is beneficial to borrowers. The objectives of increasing output and reducing unemployment are accomplished by both polices, but different groups of people benefit from the change in the interest rate, depending on whether fiscal or monetary policy is utilized to achieve these objectives. Incentives exist to influence the government's choice of policy for the same objective of increasing GDP or reducing unemployment via the policy most favorable to a particular constituency or special interest group. Here too, the rule is the same as in production theory. As long as the marginal cost is less than the marginal benefit, it is sensible to incur the cost.

In practice, and due to the influence of different constituents, governments utilize both fiscal and monetary policies jointly. In the case of the previous example, joint applications of expansionary fiscal and monetary policies will moderate their impact on the interest rate. The advantage, in addition to accommodating different constituents for political gain, is a reduction in the volatility of the interest rate, which in turn serves to stabilize the economy and improve the ability of economic agents to forecast changes in the interest rate.

Glossary

Accelerator coefficient is the magnitude of increase in investment due to a given increase in output/demand.

Annuity is a financial product with fixed stream of payments over time.

Automatic stabilizers are mechanisms that counteract and reduce the impact of business cycles.

Autonomous expenditures are expenditures that do not depend on income or production. Each sector of consumption, investment, government expenditures, and net exports is assumed to have a component that is a function of income or production and a portion that is not.

Balanced budget multiplier is the multiplier when changes in government expenditures and taxes are equal.

Barter is the exchange of one thing for another when neither good is "money."

Business cycle is the collection of peaks and troughs of the economy.

Consumer surplus is the sum of the differences between the market-clearing price and the maximum price that each consumer is willing and able to pay.

Crowding out refers to increase in interest rate as a result of expansionary fiscal policy.

Depression is a severe case of economic recession.

Disposable income is gross income minus taxes plus transfer payment.

Easy money refers to abundance of money and credit at low interest rate.

Economy of scale exists when the long-run average cost is declining, that is per unit cost declines as output increases.

Effective demand is the value of aggregate demand at the point it intersects with aggregate supply.

An **ergodic** process is a process that can be predicted by sampling.

Equilibrium refers to a point where market forces cancel each other out and there is no endogenous force left to influence the market.

Externalities are consequences, both positive and negative, that were not brought about by one's own choice and action.

Fiscal policy refers to government intervention in the economy through manipulation of government revenues and disbursements for the purpose of influencing the course of the economy.

Gross domestic product (GDP) is the value of final goods and services produced in a country in one year.

Gross national product (GNP) is the market value of final goods and services produced by the citizens of a country.

Gross substitution is the spillover from adjustments in one market, e.g., money market, into another market, e.g., goods market, by substituting expenditure from one form, i.e., goods and services, to another form, i.e., money and assets.

Inside lag is the time between recognition of the need for a stimulus or restraint and the legislation of the appropriate regulations.

Internal rate of return of an investment is the rate of interest that would equate the discounted present value of the expected future yields to the cost of investment.

IS schedule is the loci of interest rate-output sets for which the goods market is in equilibrium.

Laissez faire et laissez passer is a doctrine that opposes government intervention in economic affairs, except for the maintenance of property rights.

Liquidity trap is an economic situation in which investment does not respond to interest rate decline initiated by an increase in the supply of money.

LM schedule is the loci of combinations of interest rates and incomes that result in equilibrium in the money market.

Macroeconomics is the study of aggregated indicators, such as gross domestic product (GDP).

Marginal efficiency of capital is the discount rate that would make the present value of a series of income from investment during its life equal to its supply price.

Marginal propensity to consume is the change in consumption due to one unit change in income.

Money illusion indicates that economic agents make decisions based on nominal rather than real variables.

Monetary policy refers to government intervention in the economy through manipulation of supply of money for the purpose of influencing the course of the economy.

Monopoly is a market structure in which a single producer provides the good or the service.

Multiplier effect refers to the successive rounds of income-consumption generated by an initial increase in consumption, investment, or government expenditures.

Money is said to be **neutral** when changes in stock of money only affects nominal but not real variables.

Outside lag is the time between a policy action and the appearance of its effects in the economy.

Pareto optimal distribution is a distribution in which no one can be made better-off without making someone else worse-off.

Pigou effect is the hypothesis that a reduction in prices results in a wealth effect that is sufficient to increase aggregate demand to the full employment level, thus eliminating the Keynesian possibility of equilibrium in goods and money markets with persistent unemployment.

Portfolio motive or speculative motive represents the portion of demand for money beyond the demand for the purpose of transactions.

Present value of future income is the amount of money that, if lent at the current interest rate, would result in the same amount of income in the future as the income that was targeted.

Producer surplus is the sum of the difference between the market-clearing price and the minimum price that each producer is willing and able to charge.

Recession refers to an overall decline of the economy. In the United States a recession is declared when GDP declines for two consecutive quarters.

Say's law of market states that production creates its demand.

Tight money refers to shortage of money and credit and the presence of interest rate.

Transfer payment is any payment made by the government to the private sector.

Unemployment refers to an economic condition in which there are people who are actively seeking employment at the prevailing market wage but cannot find a job.

Notes

Chapter 1

1. Frisch (1993).
2. Hume (1748 [2005]).
3. Fisher (1907), pp. 18–27.
4. Fisher (1933), pp. 337–257.
5. Wicksell (1958).
6. Owen (1817); Sismondi (1819 [1991]).
7. Marx (1867 [2007]).
8. Marx (1867 [2007]).
9. Naghshpour (2013b).
10. Patinkin (1954), pp. 113–128.
11. Smith (1776 [2011]).
12. Fisher (1907), pp. 18–27.
13. Marx (1867 [2007]).

Chapter 2

1. Keynes (1936 [2006]).
2. Naghshpour (2013b).
3. Friedman and Schwartz (1963).
4. Wicker (1966).
5. Brunner and Meltzer (1968).
6. Epstein and Ferguson (1984), pp. 957–983.
7. Anderson, Shughart, and Tollison (1988), pp. 3–23.
8. Hayek (1932).
9. Keynes (1936 [2006]).
10. Friedman and Schwartz (1963).
11. Naghshpour (2013b).
12. Keynes (1936 [2006]).
13. Tobin (1958), pp. 65–86.
14. Tobin (1958), pp. 65–86.
15. Tobin (1958), pp. 65–86.
16. Keynes (1936 [2006]).
17. Keynes (1936 [2006]).
18. Friedman (1961), pp. 447–466.

Chapter 3

1. Naghshpour (2013a).
2. Naghshpour (2013a).

Chapter 4

1. Naghshpour (2013a).
2. Keynes (1936 [2006]).
3. Marshall (1890 [2012]).
4. Keynes (1936 [2006]).

Chapter 5

1. Friedman (1956).
2. Naghshpour (2013b).
3. Keynes (1936 [2006]).
4. Marshall (1890 [2012]).
5. Keynes (1936 [2006]).
6. Clower (1965).
7. Barro and Grossman (1976).
8. Malinvaud (1977).
9. Tobin (1958).
10. Fellner (1948).
11. Meltzer (1963).
12. Ando and Modigliani (1965).
13. Hanes (2006).
14. Pollin (2012).
15. Ueda (2012).

Chapter 6

1. Pigou (1943).
2. Pigou (1943).
3. Tobin (1980).
4. Naghshpour (2013b).
5. Pesek and Saving (1967).
6. Johnson (1969).
7. Pigou (1943).

8. Gordon and Leeper (2005).
9. Cassou and Lansing (1996).
10. Diebold and Rudebusch (1992).
11. Romer (1999).
12. Christiano and Harrison (1996).
13. Cohen and Follette (2000).

Chapter 7

1. Keynes (1936 [2006]).
2. Hammond (2011), pp. 643–660.
3. Friedman (1956); Friedman (1959), pp. 327–351.
4. Muth (1961).
5. Lucas (1972), pp. 103–124.
6. Sargent's (1979).
7. Tobin (1996).
8. Lucas (1972), pp. 103–124.
9. Keynes (1936 [2006]).
10. Lucas (1972), pp. 103–124.
11. Lucas (1972), pp. 103–124.
12. Mankiw (1985), pp. 529–538.
13. Akerlof and Yellen (1985), pp. 823–838.
14. Blanchard and Kiyotaki (1985).
15. Naghshpour (2013b).
16. Friedman (1960).
17. Ball, Mankiw, and Romer (1988), pp. 1–90.
18. Kydland and Prescott (1982), pp. 1345–1370.
19. Friedman (1968).
20. Lucas (1978), pp. 353–357.
21. Tobin (1980).
22. Schumpeter (1939).
23. Wicksell (1958).
24. Naghshpour (2013a).
25. Wicksell (1958).
26. Samuelson (1939).
27. Bronfenbrenner (1969).
28. Blinder (1979).
29. Tobin (1987).
30. Friedman (1968).
31. Lucas (1990), pp. 293–316.

32. Feldstein (1986), pp. 26–30.
33. Samuelson (1984), p. 4; Tobin (1987).

Chapter 8

1. Naghshpour (2013b).
2. Gordon (1997), pp. 11–32.
3. Tobin (1996).
4. Arestis and Sawyer (2004), pp. 441–463.
5. Friedman and Heller (1969).
6. Hicks (1974).
7. Robinson (1933).
8. Chamberlin (1933).
9. Mankiw (1985), pp. 529–538.
10. Akerlof and Yellen (1985), pp. 823–838.
11. Mankiw (1985), pp. 529–538.
12. Gordon (1997).
13. Blanchard and Kiyotaki (1985).
14. Marshall (1890 [2012]).
15. Akerlof and Yellen (1985), pp. 823–838.

Chapter 9

1. Keynes (1936 [2006]).
2. Eichner and Kregel (1975).
3. Keynes (1936 [2006]).
4. Naghshpour (2013b).
5. Arrow and Hahn (1971).
6. Keynes (1937), pp. 209–223.
7. Davidson (1978); Davidson (1982), pp. 182–198.
8. Davidson (2001).
9. Davidson (1978); Davidson (1982), pp. 182–198.
10. Leijonhufvud (1968).
11. Robinson (1933).

Chapter 10

1. Friedman (1956).
2. Ando and Modigliani (1953), pp. 55–84.
3. Brumberg (1956), pp. 66–72.

4. Modigliani and Brumberg (1980).
5. Ando and Modigliani (1965).
6. Barro (1974).
7. Buiter and Tobin (1976).
8. Phillips (1958), pp. 283–299.
9. Gali et al. (2005).
10. Taylor (1980), pp. 1–23.
11. Calvo (1983), pp. 383–398.
12. Rudd and Whelan (2001).
13. Galie and Gertler (1999), pp. 195–222.
14. Galie and Gertler (1999), pp. 195–222.
15. Fuhrer and Moore (1995), pp. 127–160.
16. Mankiw and Reis (2002), pp. 1295–1328.
17. Ball (1994), pp. 282–289.
18. Moore (1979), pp. 49–70.
19. Cutler (1991), pp. 273–280.
20. Moore (1979), pp. 49–70.
21. Moore (1979), pp. 49–70.
22. Keynes (1930 [1976]).
23. Blinder et al. (1998).
24. Skott and Zipperer (2010).
25. Mankiw (1985), pp. 529–538.
26. Akerlof and Yellen (1985), pp. 823–838.
27. Blanchard and Kiyotaki (1985).
28. McCallum (1986).
29. Defina (1991).
30. Ball, Mankiw, and Romer (1988), pp. 1–90.
31. Lucas (1973), pp. 326–334.
32. Akerlof, Rose, and Yellen (1988), pp. 66–75.
33. Barro (1974).
34. Feldstein (1982), pp. 1–20.
35. Johnson (1987), pp. 435–453.
36. Evans (1985), pp. 243–252.
37. Kroy and McMillin (1987), pp. 15–19.
38. Vaughn and Wagner (1992), pp. 37–49.
39. Dalamagas (1993), pp. 129–146.
40. Friedman and Meiselman (1963).
41. Ando and Modigliani (1965), pp. 693–728.
42. Ando and Modigliani (1965), pp. 693–728.
43. DePrano and Mayor (1965), pp. 729–752.
44. Hamburger (1977), pp. 265–288.

45. Moore (1979), pp. 49–70.
46. Arestis and Sawyer (2004), pp. 441–463.
47. Naghshpour (2013a).
48. Clark (2001), pp. 403–436.

Chapter 11

1. DePrano and Mayer (1965), pp. 729–752.

References

Akerlof, G. A., & Yellen, J. L. (1985). A near—rational model of the business cycle, with wage and price inertia. *Quarterly Journal of Economics 100*(Supplement), 823–838.

Akerlof, G. A., Rose, A., & Yellen, J. L. (1988). The new keynesian economics and the output-inflation trade-off: Comment. *Brookings Papers on Economic Activity 1988*(1), 66–75.

Anderson, G. M., Shughart II, W. F., & Tollison, R. D. (1988). A public choice theory of the great contraction. *Public Choice 59,* 3–23.

Ando, A., & Modigliani, F. (1953). The "Life-Cycle" hypothesis of saving: Aggregate implications and tests. *American Economic Review 53*(1), 55–84.

Ando, A., & Modigliani, F. (1965). The relative stability of monetary velocity and the investment multiplier. *The American Economic Review 55*(4), 693–728.

Arestis, P., & Sawyer, M. C. (2004). On the effectiveness of monetary policy and of fiscal policy. *Review of Social Economy 62*(4), 441–463.

Arrow, K. J., & Hahn, F. H. (1971). *General Equilibrium Analysis*. San Francisco, CA: Holden-Day.

Ball, L. (1994). Credible disinflation with staggered price settings. *American Economic Review 84*(1), 282–289.

Ball, L., Mankiw, N. G., & Romer, D. (1988). The new economics and the output-inflation trade off. *Brookings Papers on Economic Activity 1988*(1), 1–90.

Barro, R. J. (1974). Are government bonds net wealth? *Journal of Political Economy 82*(6), 1095–117.

Barro, R. J., & Grossman, H. I. (1976). *Money, employment, and inflation.* Cambridge: Cambridge University Press.

Blanchard, O. J., & Kiyotaki, N. (1985). *Monopolistic competition, aggregate demand externalities and real effects of nominal money, Working Paper.* Cambridge, MA: MIT.

Blinder, A. S. (1979). *Economic policy and the great stagflation.* London, UK: Macmillan.

Blinder, A. S., Canetti, E. D., Lebow, D. E., & Rudd, J. B. (1998). *Asking about prices: A new approach to understanding price stickiness.* New York, NY: Russell Sage Foundation.

Bronfenbrenner, M. (1969). *Is the business cycle obsolete?* New York, NY: J. Wiley and Sons.

Brumberg, R. E. (1956). An approximation to the aggregate saving function. *Economic Journal 46,* 66–72.

Brunner, K., & Meltzer, A. H. (1968). Liquifity Traps for Money, Bank Credit, and Interest Rates. *Tepper School of Business*. Paper 605.

Buiter, W., & Tobin, J. (1976). Long run effects of fiscal and monetary policy on aggregate demand. In J. Stein (Ed.), *Monetarism: Studies in monetary economics* (*Vol. 1*). Amsterdam, NL: North-Holland.

Calvo, G. A. (1983). Staggered prices in a utility maximizing framework. *Journal of Monetary Economics 12*, 383–398.

Cassou, S. P., & Lansing, K. J. (1996). *Welfare, stabilization, or growth: A comparison of different fiscal objectives.* San Francisco, CA: Working Paper No. 9614 Federal Reserve Board.

Christiano, L. J., & Harrison, S. G. (1996). Chaos, sunspots, and automatic stabilizers. NBER Working Paper No. 5703. National Bureau of Economic Research. *Journal of Monetary Economics 44*(1), 3–31.

Clark, G. (2001). Debt, deficits, and crowding out: England, 1727–1840. *European Review of Economic History 5*(3), 403–436.

Clower, R. W. (1965). The Keynesian Counter-Revolution: A Theoretical appraisal. In F.H. Hahn and F. Brechling, eds. *The Theory of Interest Rates*. London: MacMillian.

Cohen, D., & Follette, G. (2000). The automatic fiscal stabilizers: Quietly doing their thing. *Federal Reserve Bank of New York Economic Policy Review 6*, 3–68.

Cutler, H. (1991). Post keynesian monetary theory: Contrary empirical evidence. *Eastern Economic Journal 17*(3), 273–280.

Dalamagas, B. A. (1993). Fiscal effectiveness and debt illusion in a rational expectations model. *Annales D'Economie Et De Statistique 31*, 129–146.

Davidson, P. (1978). *Money and the real world.* London, UK: Macmillan.

Davidson, P. (1982). Rational expectations: A fallacious foundation for studying crucial decision—Making processes. *Journal of Post Keynesian Economics 5*(2), 182–198.

Davisdon, P. (2001). Monetary policy in the twenty-first century in the light of the debate between charlatism and monetarism. In J. E. Biddle, J. B. Davis, and S. Medema (Eds.), *Economics broadly considered: Essays in honour of Warren J. Samuels*. New York, NY: Routledge.

DeFina, R. H. (1991). Does *Inflation Depress the Stock Market*. Philadelphia: Federal Reserve Bank of Philadelphia.

DePrano, M., & Mayer, T. (1965). Test of the relative importance of autonomous expenditures and money. *American Economic Association 55*(4), 729–752.

Diebold, F., & Rudebusch, G. (1992). Have postwar economic fluctuations been stabilized? *American Economic Review 82*, 993–1005.

Eichner, A. S., & Kregel, J. A. (1975). An essay on Post-Keynesian theory: A new paradigm in economics. *The Journal of Economic Literature 13*(4), 1293–1314.

Epstein, G., & Ferguson, T. (1984). Monetary policy, loan liquidation, and industrial conflict: The federal reserve and the open market operations of 1932. *Journal of Economic History 44*(4), 957–983.

Evans, P. (1985). Utility profits, fiscal illusion and local public expenditures. *Public Choice 38*, 243–252.

Feldstein, M. (1982). Government deficits and aggregate demand. *Journal of Monetary Economics 9*, 1–20.

Feldstein, M. (1986). Supply-Side economics: Old truth and new claims. *American Economic Review 76*(2), 26–30.

Fellner, W. (1948). Average-cost pricing and the theory of uncertainty. *The Journal of Political Economy 56*(3), 249–252.

Fisher, I. (1907). Why has the doctrine of laissez faire been abandoned? *Science New Series 25*(627), 18–27.

Fisher, I. (1933). The debt-deflation theory of great depressions. *Econometrica 1*(4), 337–257.

Friedman, M. (1956). The quantity theory of money, a restatement. In M. Friedman (Ed.), *Studies in the quantity theory of money.* Chicago, US: University of Chicago Press.

Friedman, M. (1959). The demand for money: Some theoretical and empirical results. *Journal of Political Economy 67*, 327–351.

Friedman, M. (1960). *A Program for monetary stability* (Vol. 541). New York: Fordham University Press.

Friedman, M. (1961). The lag effect of monetary policy. *Journal of Political Economy 69*(5), 447–466.

Friedman, M. (1968). *Dollars and deficits.* Englewood, NJ: Prentice-Hall.

Friedman, M., & Meiselman, D. (1963). *The Relative Stability of the Investment Multiplier and Monetary Velocity in the United States, 1897–1958. Stabilization Policies.* Englewood Cliffs, NJ: Prentice-Hall.

Friedman, M., & Schwartz, A. L. (1963). *A monetary history of the United States, 1867–1960.* Trenton, NJ: Princeton University Press.

Frisch, R. (1933). Propagation problems and impulse problems in dynamic economics. Copenhagen, DK: Universitets Okonomiske Institutt, Publikasion nr. 3.

Fuhrer, J., & Moore, G. (1995). Inflation persistence. *Quarterly Journal of Economics 110*, 127–160.

Galie, J., & Gertler, M. (1999). Inflation dynamics: A structural econometric analysis. *Journal of Monetary Economics 44*, 195–222.

Gali, J., Gertler, M., & Lopez-Salido, D. (2005). Robustness of the estimates of the hybrid new Keynesian Phillips curve. National Bureau of Economic Research, Working Paper No. 11788, 1–15. *Journal of Monetary Economics 52*(6), 1107–1118.

Gordon, R. J. (1990). Front matter to "The Measurement of Durable Goods Prices". In *The measurement of durable goods prices* (pp. 19–4). University of Chicago Press, 1990.

Gordon, R. J. (1997). The time-varying NAIRU and its implications for economic policy. *Journal of Economic Perspectives 11*(1), 11–32.

Gordon, D. B., & Leeper, E. M. (2005). *Are countercyclical fiscal policies counterproductive?* (Working Paper No. 11869: 1–32.). Cambridge, MA: National Bureau of Economic Research.

Hamburger, M. J. (1977). Behavior of the money stock: Is there a puzzle? *Journal of Monetary Economics 3*, 265–288.

Hammond, J. D. (2011). Friedman and samuelson on the business cycle. *Cato Journal 31*(3), 643–660.

Hanes, C. (2006). The kiquidity trap and US interest rates in the 1930s. *Journal of Money, Credit, and Banking 38*(1), 163–194.

Hayek, F. A. (1932). A note on the development of the doctrine of forced saving. *The Quarterly Journal of Economics, 47*(1), 123–133.

Hicks, J. (1974). Capital controversies: Ancient and modern. *The American Economic Review 64*(2), 307–316.

Hume, D. (1748 [2005]). *Essays, moral, political, and literary.* Retrieved September 11, 2005, from Indianapolis: The Online Library of Liberty: http://files.libertyfund.org/files/704/Hume_0059.pdf#page=4

Johnson, D. (1987). Are government bonds net wealth?: Intertemporal optimization and government budget constraint. *Journal of Macroeconomics 8*, 435–453.

Johnson, H. G. (1969). Inside money, outside money, income, wealth and welfare in monetary theory. *Journal of Money, Credit, and Banking 1*(1), 30–45.

Keynes, J. M. (1930 [1976]). *A treatise on money.* Brooklyn, NY: Ams Pr Inc.

Keynes, J. M. (1936 [2006]). *The general theory of employment, interest and money.* Delhi, IN: Atlantic Publishers and Distributors.

Keynes, J. M. (1937). The general theory of employment. *Quarterly Journal of Economics 51*(2), 209–223.

Kroy, F. D., & McMillin, W. (1987). The ricardian rquivalence hypothesis. *Economic Letters 25*, 15–19.

Kydland, F. E., & Prescott, E. C. (1982). Time to build and aggregate fluctuations. *Econometrica 50*(6), 1345–1370.

Leijonhufvud, A. (1968). *On keynesian economics and the economics of keynes.* London, UK: Oxford University Press.

Lucas, R. E. (1972). Expectations and the neutrality of money. *Journal of Economic Theory 4*(2), 103–124.

Lucas, R. E. (1973). Some international evidence on output-inflation trade-offs. *American Economic Review 63*, 326–334.

Lucas, R. E. (1978). Unemployment policy. *American Economic Review. 68*(2), 353–357.

Lucas, R. E. (1990). Supply-side economics: An analytical review. *Oxford Economic Papers 42*(2), 293–316.

Malinvaud, E. (1977). *The theory of economic unemployment revisited.* Oxford: Blackwell.

Mankiw, N. G. (1985). Small menu costs and large business cycles: A macroeconomic model of monopoly. *Quarterly Journal of Economics 100*(2), 529–538.

Mankiw, N. G., & Reis, R. (2002). Sticky information versus sticky prices: A proposal to replace the new keynesian phillips curve. *The Quarterly Journal of Economics 117*, 1295–1328.

Marshall, A. (1890 [2012]). *Principles of economics.* New York, NY: Digireads.com

Marx, K. (1867 [2007]). *Das kapital.* Synergy International of the Americas, Ltd. Washington D.C.

McCallum, B. T. (1986). *Monetry vs. Fiscal Policy Effects: A Review of the Debate.* Cambridge, MA: National Bureau of Economic Research.

Meltzer, A. H. (1963) Yet Another Look at the Low Level Liquidity Trap. *Econometrica 31*(3), 545–549.

Modigliani, F., & Brumberg, R. E.(1980). Utility analysis and the consumption function: An attempt at a integration. In A. Abel (Ed.), *The collective papers of Franco Modigliani: The life cycle hypothesis of savings* (Vol. 2). (128–197). Cambridge, MA: MIT Press.

Moore, B. J. (1979). The endogenous money stock. *Journal of Post Keynesian Economics 2*(1), 49–70.

Muth, J. F. (1961). Rational expectations and the theory of price movement. *Econometrica 29*(3), 315–335.

Naghshpour, S. (2013a). *Monetary policy: Government intervention to influence market performance.* New York, NY: Business Expert Press.

Naghshpour, S. (2013b). *The fundamentals of money and financial systems.* New York, NY: Business Expert Press.

Owen, R. D. (1817). Report to the committee for the relief of the manufacturing poor. In *The life of Robert Owen* (2012). Ulan Press.

Patinkin, D. (1954). Dichotomies of the pricing process in economic theory. *Economica 21*(82), 113–128.

Pesek, K. A., & Saving, T. R. (1967). *Money, wealth and economic theory.* London, UK: Macmillan.

Phillips, A. W. (1958). The Relationship between unemployment and the rate of change of money wages in the United Kingdom 1861–1957. *Economica 25*, 283–299.

Pigou, A. C. (1943). The classical stationary state. *Economic Journal 53*, 343–351.

Pollin, R. (2012). "The Great US Liquidity Trap of 2009–11: Are We Stuck Pushing on Strings?" Working Paper No 284. Political Economy Research Institute.

Robinson, J. V. (1933). *The economics of imperfect competition.* London, UK: Macmillan.

Romer, C. (1999). Changes in business cycles: Evidence and explanation. *Journal of Economic Perspectives 13*(2), 23–44.

Rudd, J., & Whelan, K. (2001). *New tests of the new-keynesian Phillips curve.* Washington, D.C.: Federal Reserve Board.

Samuelson, P. A. (1984). Evaluating reagonomics. *Challenge 27*(5), 4.

Sargent, T. J. (1979). *Macroeconomic theory-Economic Theory, Econometrics, and mathematical models.* New York: Academic Press.

Schumpeter, J. A. (1939). *Business cycles: A theoretical, historical and statistical analysis of the capitalist process.* New York: McGraw Hill.

Sismondi, J. C. L. (1819 [1991]). *New principles of political economy.* C. R. Hyse (Ed.). Piscataway, NJ: Transaction Publishers.

Skott, P., & Zipperer, B. (2010). An empirical evaluation of three post keynesian models. Amherst, MA: University of Massachusetts.

Smith, A. (1776 [2011]). *Wealth of nations.* Books IV—V. London, UK: Methuen & Co., Ltd., Create Space Independent Publishing Platform.

Taylor, J. B. (1980). Aggregate dynamics and staggered contract. *Journal of Political Economy 88,* 1–23.

Tobin, J. (1958). Liquidity preference as behavior towards risk. *Review of Economic Studies 25,* 65–86.

Tobin, J. (1980). *Asset accumulation and economic activity: Reflections on contemporary macroeconomic theory.* Oxford, EN: Basil Blackwell.

Tobin, J. (1987). *Policies for prosperity: Essays in a keynesian mode.* P. M. Jackson (Ed.). Brighton, EN: Wheatsheaf.

Tobin, J. (1996). *Full employment and growth: Ruther essays on policy.* Cheltenham. UK and Brookfield, USA: Edward Elgar.

U.S. Department of Commerce Bureau of Economic Analysis. (2013). *Glossary.* Retrieved April 2, 2013, from http://www.bea.gov/glossary/glossary.cfm?key_word=GNP&letter=G

Ueda, Z. (2012). Deleveraging and monetary policy: Japan since the 1990s and the United States since 2007. *The Journal of Economic Perspecties 26*(3), 177–201.

Vaughn, K. I., & Wagner, R. E. (1992). Public debt controversies: An essay in reconciliation. *Kyklos 45,* 37–49.

Wicker, E. R. (1966). *Federal Reserve Monetary Policy, 1917–1933.* New York, NY: Random House.

Wicksell, K. (1958). Ends and means in economics. In E. Lindahl (Ed.). London, UK: Allen and Unwin, Selected Papers on Economic Theory.

Index

OTHER TITLES FROM THE ECONOMICS COLLECTION

Philip Romero, The University of Oregon and Jeffrey Edwards,
North Carolina A&T State University, Editors

- *Managerial Economics: Concepts and Principles* by Donald Stengel
- *Your Macroeconomic Edge: Investing Strategies for the Post-Recession World* by Philip J. Romero
- *Working with Economic Indicators: Interpretation and Sources* by Donald Stengel
- *Innovative Pricing Strategies to Increase Profits* by Daniel Marburger
- *Regression for Economics* by Shahdad Naghshpour
- *Statistics for Economics* by Shahdad Naghshpour
- *How Strong Is Your Firm's Competitive Advantage?* by Daniel Marburger
- *A Primer on Microeconomics* by Thomas Beveridge
- *Game Theory: Anticipating Reactions for Winning Actions* by Mark L. Burkey
- *A Primer on Macroeconomics* by Thomas Beveridge
- *Economic Decision Making Using Cost Data: A Guide for Managers* by Daniel Marburger
- *The Fundamentals of Money and Financial Systems* by Shahdad Naghshpour
- *International Economics: Understanding the Forces of Globalization for Managers* by Paul Torelli
- *The Economics of Crime* by Zagros Madjd-Sadjadi
- *Money and Banking: An Intermediate Market-Based Approach* by William D. Gerdes

Announcing the Business Expert Press Digital Library

*Concise E-books Business Students Need
for Classroom and Research*

This book can also be purchased in an e-book collection by your library as
- a one-time purchase,
- that is owned forever,
- allows for simultaneous readers,
- has no restrictions on printing, and
- can be downloaded as PDFs from within the library community.

Our digital library collections are a great solution to beat the rising cost of textbooks. e-books can be loaded into their course management systems or onto student's e-book readers.

The **Business Expert Press** digital libraries are very affordable, with no obligation to buy in future years. For more information, please visit **www.businessexpertpress.com/librarians**. To set up a trial in the United States, please contact **Adam Chesler** at *adam.chesler@ businessexpertpress.com* for all other regions, contact **Nicole Lee** at *nicole.lee@igroupnet.com*.

www.ingramcontent.com/pod-product-compliance
Lightning Source LLC
Chambersburg PA
CBHW070922270326
41927CB00011B/2683